FORCES AT WORK

Macmill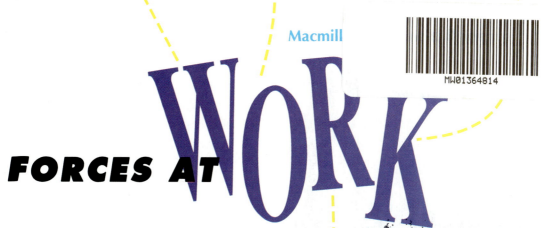

AUTHORS

Mary Atwater
The University of Georgia

Prentice Baptiste
University of Houston

Lucy Daniel
Rutherford County Schools

Jay Hackett
University of Northern Colorado

Richard Moyer
University of Michigan, Dearborn

Carol Takemoto
Los Angeles Unified School District

Nancy Wilson
Sacramento Unified School District

Volcanic forces in action

**Macmillan/McGraw-Hill
School Publishing Company
New York   Columbus**

MACMILLAN / McGRAW-HILL

CONSULTANTS

Assessment:
Mary Hamm
Associate Professor
Department of Elementary Education
San Francisco State University
San Francisco, CA

Cognitive Development:
Pat Guild, Ed.D.
Director, Graduate Programs in Education and Learning Styles Consultant
Antioch University
Seattle, WA

Kathi Hand, M.A.Ed.
Middle School Teacher and Learning Styles Consultant
Assumption School
Seattle, WA

Derrick R. Lavoie
Assistant Professor of Science Education
Montana State University
Bozeman, MT

Earth Science:
David G. Futch
Associate Professor of Biology
San Diego State University
San Diego, CA

Dr. Shadia Rifai Habbal
Harvard-Smithsonian Center for Astrophysics
Cambridge, MA

Tom Murphree, Ph.D.
Global Systems Studies
Monterey, CA

Suzanne O'Connell
Assistant Professor
Wesleyan University
Middletown, CT

Sidney E. White
Professor of Geology
The Ohio State University
Columbus, OH

Environmental Education:
Cheryl Charles, Ph.D.
Executive Director
Project Wild
Boulder, CO

Gifted:
Dr. James A. Curry
Associate Professor, Graduate Faculty
College of Education, University of Southern Maine
Gorham, ME

Global Education:
M. Eugene Gilliom
Professor of Social Studies and Global Education
The Ohio State University
Columbus, OH

Life Science:
Wyatt W. Anderson
Professor of Genetics
University of Georgia
Athens, GA

Orin G. Gelderloos
Professor of Biology and Professor of Environmental Studies
University of Michigan—Dearborn
Dearborn, MI

Donald C. Lisowy
Education Specialist
New York, NY

Dr. E.K. Merrill
Assistant Professor
University of Wisconsin Center—Rock County
Madison, WI

Literature:
Dr. Donna E. Norton
Texas A&M University
College Station, TX

Copyright © 1995 Macmillan/McGraw-Hill School Publishing Company

All rights reserved. No part of this book may be reproduced or transmitted in any form or by any means, electronic or mechanical, including photocopying, recording, or by any information storage and retrieval system, without permission in writing from the publisher.

Macmillan/McGraw-Hill School Division
10 Union Square East
New York, New York 10003
Printed in the United States of America

ISBN 0-02-276125-X /6

4 5 6 7 8 9 RRW 99 98 97 96

Mathematics:
Dr. Richard Lodholz
Parkway School District
St. Louis, MO

Middle School Specialist:
Daniel Rodriguez
Principal
Pomona, CA

Misconceptions:
Dr. Charles W. Anderson
Michigan State University
East Lansing, MI

Dr. Edward L. Smith
Michigan State University
East Lansing, MI

Multicultural:
Bernard L. Charles
Senior Vice President
Quality Education for Minorities Network
Washington, DC

Paul B. Janeczko
Poet
Hebron, MA

James R. Murphy
Math Teacher
La Guardia High School
New York, NY

Clifford E. Trafzer
Professor and Chair, Ethnic Studies
University of California, Riverside
Riverside, CA

Physical Science:
Gretchen M. Gillis
Geologist
Maxus Exploration Company
Dallas, TX

Henry C. McBay
Professor of Chemistry
Morehouse College and Clark Atlanta University
Atlanta, GA

Wendell H. Potter
Associate Professor of Physics
Department of Physics
University of California, Davis
Davis, CA

Claudia K. Viehland
Educational Consultant, Chemist
Sigma Chemical Company
St. Louis, MO

Reading:
Charles Temple, Ph.D.
Associate Professor of Education
Hobart and William Smith Colleges
Geneva, NY

Safety:
Janice Sutkus
Program Manager: Education
National Safety Council
Chicago, IL

Science Technology and Society (STS):
William C. Kyle, Jr.
Director, School Mathematics and Science Center
Purdue University
West Lafayette, IN

Social Studies:
Jean Craven
District Coordinator of Curriculum Development
Albuquerque Public Schools
Albuquerque, NM

Students Acquiring English:
Mario Ruiz
Pomona, CA

STUDENT ACTIVITY TESTERS

Alveria Henderson
Kate McGlumphy
Katherine Petzinger
John Wirtz
Sarah Wittenbrink
Andrew Duffy
Chris Higgins
Sean Pruitt
Joanna Huber
John Petzinger

FIELD TEST TEACHERS

Kathy Bowles
Landmark Middle School
Jacksonville, FL

Myra Dietz
#46 School
Rochester, NY

John Gridley
H.L. Harshman Junior High School #101
Indianapolis, IN

Annette Porter
Schenk Middle School
Madison, WI

Connie Boone
Fletcher Middle School
Jacksonville, FL

Theresa Smith
Bates Middle School
Annapolis, MD

Debbie Stamler
Sennett Middle School
Madison, WI

Margaret Tierney
Sennett Middle School
Madison, WI

Mel Pfeiffer
I.P.S. #94
Indianapolis, IN

CONTRIBUTING WRITER
Jay Gartrell

ACKNOWLEDGEMENTS

MOVING HEAVY THINGS by Jan Adkins. Copyright © 1980 by Jan Adkins. Reprinted by permission of Houghton Mifflin Company and Curtis Brown LTD. All rights reserved.

Reprinted with permission of Bradbury Press, an Affiliate of Macmillan, Inc. from *BURTON'S ZOOM ZOOM VA-ROOOM MACHINE* by Dorothy Haas. Text, Copyright © 1990 by Dorothy Haas.

Race car

FORCES AT WORK

Lessons **Themes**

Unit Introduction   Forces at Work .... **Systems and Interactions** **6**
Predict the winners of some tug-of-war contests, and investigate how the movement of matter is affected by force and mass.

1 How Do You Measure Motion? .... **Patterns of Change** **12**
You can learn to make accurate time and distance measurements to determine the winner in many contests.

2 What Is Force? .... **Systems and Interactions** ... **24**
Find out why a diver jumping off a ten-meter platform falls toward the water.

3 Can an Object Start or Stop Moving Without Help From a Force? ... **Systems and Interactions** ... **40**
What is needed to start an object moving, change its velocity, or stop its motion?

4 What Controls Acceleration? .... **Systems and Interactions** ... **56**
Can a car accelerate as fast as an airplane? Why?

5 What Are Action and Reaction Forces? .... **Systems and Interactions** ... **70**
You can learn to identify action and reaction forces.

Unit Wrap Up   Tug-of-War Contests Revisited .... **Systems and Interactions** ... **80**
After learning about various types of forces, you'll be able to predict the winning teams in the tug-of-war contests.

EXPLORE

Science Triathlon **14**
Slipping and Sliding **28**
Jet Racing Cars **42**
Rolling Along With
  a Constant Force **58**
Launching a Balloon-
  Powered Rocket **72**

TRY THIS

Moving Marbles **20**
Experience a Force **27**
Friction Music **31**
Air Resistance **35**
Moving Magnets **37**
Moving Balloons **41**
Pulling Forces **44**
Does It Bounce or Does It Bash? **64**
Wheeling Away! **71**
Design Your Own Bridge! **78**
A New Way To Move **83**

Features

Links

Literature **L**ink
Science in Literature **10**
Moving Heavy Things **38**
Burton's Zoom Zoom
  Va-ROOOM Machine **67**

Social **S**tudies **L**ink
Scientific Development **48**

Health **L**ink
If You Provide the Action,
  What's the Reaction? **77**

Language **A**rts **L**ink
Just in Time **23**

Music/**A**rt **L**ink
Friction Can Make Beautiful Music **31**

GLOBAL PERSPECTIVE

The Evolution of Sleds **39**

CAREERS

Travel Agents **17**
Structural Design Engineers **79**

SCIENCE TECHNOLOGY AND Society

Focus on Technology
Safer Cars **53**
Bicycle Helmet Laws **65**

Departments

Glossary **84**
Index **86**
Credits **88**

5

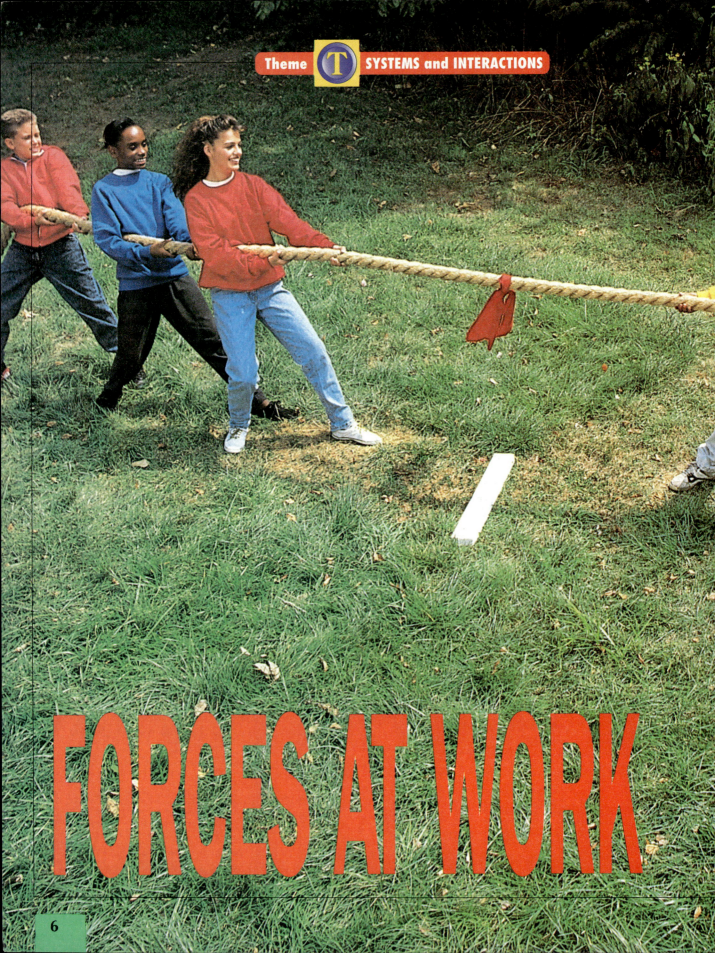

Theme **T** SYSTEMS and INTERACTIONS

FORCES AT WORK

Tug-of-war is a simple contest. Two teams hold onto a strong rope and pull in opposite directions. The winning team pulls its opponents across a marker placed on the ground between the two teams.

You've been chosen captain of a tug-of-war team. Whom do you want on your team? What determines the winner in a game of tug-of-war? What kinds of interactions between the members of each team and between the two teams are occurring? What kinds of changes in position are occurring because of these interactions?

You'll probably want to choose big, strong people for your team. But size and strength alone don't guarantee victory. The people on a tug-of-war squad all have to pull at the same time and in the same direction. Would having several very quick people on your team near the front of the rope help to get the other team moving in your direction?

When choosing a team, you may also want to consider what kind of shoes the people are wearing. Members of the soccer team who are wearing cleated shoes may be good team members, even if there are bigger people available. If the grass is slippery, soccer cleats will dig into the ground and give team members who wear them better traction.

▲ Tug-of-war between three children on roller skates and three children in shoes

If scientists were trying to predict the winners of a tug-of-war match, they would probably want to know the same kinds of things about the team members. A scientist might ask, "How much pulling force can each team produce? Which team has the greatest total mass? Which team can react the quickest? Are all the members of a team pulling in exactly the same direction?"

The total force applied to an object (that is, how fast and for how long the pushes or pulls are applied) and the mass of that object are factors that affect the motion of all matter on Earth. Whether you're observing the motions of a dead leaf carried by the wind or an ocean liner leaving a dock, all matter on Earth interacts with forces according to the same rules.

Forces affect all matter on Earth. In this unit, you'll learn how to identify and measure a force, how forces affect matter, and how matter behaves when forces are balanced (cancel each other out) and when they're not balanced. You'll learn to answer questions such as, "What started this object moving?" and "Why did it stop?"

In science classes, you're often asked to observe, hypothesize, collect and analyze data, and draw conclusions. When you do these things, you're using some of the same steps scientists use when they're doing research and experimenting. What are some steps scientists use and what do they mean?

1. **State a problem.** Many times you observe (gather information using your senses) and then ask a question about what you observe.

2. **Form a hypothesis** (hī poth´ ə sis). A hypothesis is a statement of what you think the answer to your question might be.

3. **Design an experiment.** In order for a statement to be a hypothesis, it must be able to be tested. When you design an experiment, you decide what materials and procedure you'll use to see if your hypothesis can be supported.

4. **Record and analyze data.** Any observations you make, including all measurements, must be

▲ Tug-of-war between four children and a large boulder

Tug-of-war between three children and an adult ▼

You'll be asked to use many of these steps as you work through the activities in science this year. Use some of these steps and try to predict the winners in some of the strange tug-of-war contests pictured on these pages.

Minds On! Work with two other people and use your *Activity Log* page 1 to practice using a scientific method process.

Look at the photo of the children having a tug-of-war contest with a boulder. State a problem question, such as "Will the children be able to pull the boulder across the line marker?" Next, write a hypothesis about what you think will happen. Then, decide how you could set up an experiment to test the hypothesis. What materials would you need, and what steps would you use? What observations would you make, and what data would need to be recorded? What conclusions do you think might be reached? ●

If you're aware of this process of science, you'll probably find yourself using some of the steps in everyday situations.

written down carefully and examined to aid you in drawing a conclusion.

5. Draw conclusions.
Once the data have all been gathered, they must be interpreted and compared with the hypothesis. Did the data support the hypothesis?

Usually it's not enough to have only one investigation to form a conclusion about a hypothesis. A scientist may repeat an experiment many times and may have other scientists repeat the same experiment before the results can be accepted.

9

Literature 🔗 Link

Science in Literature

In the following books, you can read how forces affect the way you interact with everything around you. The forces might be tiny—have you ever felt how little force it takes to keep a canoe gliding through calm water? Or the forces might be immense—how much force do you think it would take to start an ocean liner sliding down off its wooden supports into the water? But big or small, forces are everywhere, interacting with you in lots of ways. Let's see if you can recognize some of the ways forces affect your life. Do any of the situations mentioned in the books on these two pages sound familiar?

Moving Heavy Things by Jan Adkins.
Boston: Houghton Mifflin, 1980.

People have been lifting and carrying enormously heavy things since long before the Pyramids were being constructed. How do they do it? This book both tells and shows some little-known secrets of the moving business. Did you know that a strap around your forehead can make carrying a canoe easier? How would you knot a rope to hoist or lower an unconscious person to safety? This well-illustrated handbook makes tricky lifting problems simple. Once you've read it, you'll never mind a heavy load again.

Burton's Zoom Zoom Va-ROOOM Machine by Dorothy Haas.
New York: Bradbury Press, 1990.

Have you ever dreamed of inventing a wonderful new device that would make you rich and famous? Burton invents things all through this novel, although spies lurk and enemies glare. Burton and his friends confuse all the schemes of the bad guys; Burton's family (all inventors, too) have successes and surprises of their own; and best of all, Burton's newest invention will soon be carrying kids all over the world. Of course we can't tell you much about Burton's secret invention, but here's a clue: what has skateboard wheels and rocket wings?

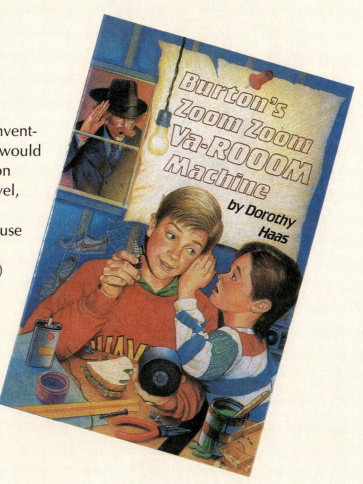

Other Good Books To Read

▲ **Which Way Is Up? by Gail Kay Haines. New York: Atheneum, 1987.**

What is gravity, anyway? This book with its well-drawn pictures and simple, clear explanations will help you understand once and for all the scientific meaning for words like *up, down, weight, mass,* and many others. Even Einstein's gravitons are introduced.

▲ **The Way Things Work by David Macaulay. Boston: Houghton Mifflin, 1988.**

You'll come back to this wonderful book again and again to see how more pieces of technology work. The telephone, the computer, the jet airplane, the tape recorder, the robot—it's an endless list. Macaulay's drawings do even more than his words to make the explanations clear.

▲ **The Hidden World of Forces by Jack R. White. New York: Dodd, Mead & Company, 1987.**

Forces are at work all around us. They make heavy jets stay up, they let a knife cut a sandwich, they help us grasp a glass of water and lift it to our faces. The universe is full of matter invisible forces control. This book makes the invisible understandable.

Theme **T** PATTERNS of CHANGE

How Do You Measure Motion?

What changes when something moves? How can you tell how fast something is moving? You can move, and objects all around you can move, but how can movement be measured? In this lesson you'll explore motion, speed, velocity, acceleration, and how to measure movement on Earth.

Who'll Be First to the Finish Line?

Imagine dashing into cold ocean water with a group of 1,200 swimmers. You are beginning a triathlon and will be racing with the other triathletes nonstop for almost nine hours. The finish line is 225 kilometers (about 140 miles) away! Will you be the new champion?

Triathlons are three-part races that last all day. Women and men competing in a triathlon race toward the finish line by swimming 4 kilo-

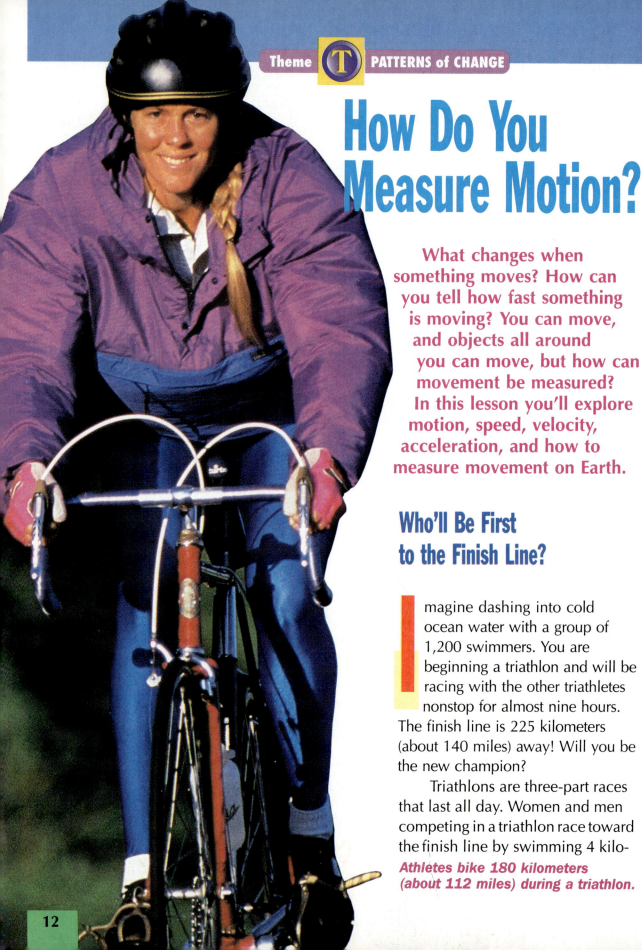

Athletes bike 180 kilometers (about 112 miles) during a triathlon.

meters (about 2.5 miles), then bicycling 180 kilometers (about 112 miles), and finally running a full marathon of 42 kilometers (26 miles). The winner is the first person to finish all three events.

Top triathletes can complete these races in about nine hours. Remember, there are three parts to a triathlon—swimming, biking, and running. How much do you think triathletes' speeds change when they switch from swimming to bicycling and from bicycling to running? Can you swim as fast as you run or run as fast as you bike?

Hundreds of swimmers begin racing at the start of a triathlon.

Minds On! Get together in groups of four to try to predict how much faster each of you can run than swim and how much faster each of you can bike than run. ●

Before entering a triathlon, athletes check the exact distances to be covered and the time the race should last. Knowing the usual speeds of other competitors in a race may help an athlete find a winning strategy. Athletes must also be certain they know the direction they should travel on the course. They can't win if they get lost!

Minds On! Scientists who study moving objects need to make accurate measurements of time and distance. Accurate time and distance measurements are also needed to determine the winner in many sports contests.

In your **Activity Log** page 2, list several different contests where the distance that something moves, rather than the time it takes, determines the winner (for example, the shot put).

In your **Activity Log**, list several sporting events in which the winner is the person who moves a measured distance in the shortest time (for example, a 100-meter dash).

During a fire drill, moving the distance from your classroom to an exit in a short period of time is important for your safety. List in your **Activity Log** several other examples of everyday tasks where time and distance are important. ●

The winner of a triathlon is the first person to cross the finish line and break the tape.

EXPLORE Activity!

Science Triathlon

"How long will it take us to get to the store from your house? Should we take the short cut? If you ride your skateboard, can you keep up with my bicycle?" You answer questions like these every day. You probably can estimate travel time, distance, direction, and speed very well. But sometimes you need a more exact measure of an object's speed. In this activity, you'll calculate several average speeds in a Science Triathlon.

What You Need

stopwatch
meterstick
masking tape
Activity Log pages 3–4

What To Do

1. Use masking tape to mark a starting line on the floor. Measure 10 m from the starting line and mark this as the finish line. This will be your racecourse. Choose a racer, a timer, and a recorder.

2. The racer should stand a few meters behind the starting line. At the start signal, the racer begins to walk at a normal speed to the finish line. When the racer crosses the starting line, the timer times the race to the finish line.

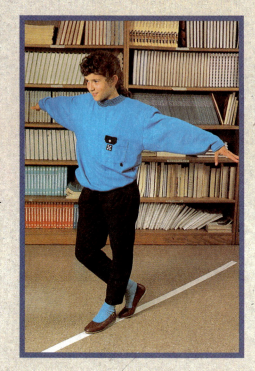

3 Record the number of seconds it takes the racer to walk 10 m in the data table in the **Activity Log**. Repeat this "walk" 2 more times and record these data.

Add these 3 times together and divide the sum by 3 to find the average time it takes this racer to walk 10 m. Record.

4 Switch roles. Now determine how long it will take a new racer to run 10 m. The racer should run from several steps behind the starting line to the finish line when the start signal is given. Run the course 2 more times. Calculate and record the average time.

5 Switch roles again so that everyone has a new role. Complete the science triathlon with a race. The racer must touch the toe of one foot to the heel of the other foot on each step down the 10-m race-course. Do this 3 times. Calculate and record the average time.

What Happened?
1. Which race had the shortest average time? The longest?
2. Use the average times you calculated to find the speed for each race. You can do this by dividing the distance moved (10 m) by the average time it took to cover the distance.

$$\text{Speed} = \frac{\text{distance moved}}{\text{average time}}$$

What was the speed in m/s for the walking race? For the running race? For the walking-toe-to-heel race?

What Now?
1. How long would it take to complete a nonstop Science Triathlon by walking 10 m, running 10 m, and toe-to-heel walking 10 m? What do you predict would be the average speed for the entire 30 m? Test your prediction by calculating the total time required and then dividing the total distance of 30 m by this time. Now have one team member complete the entire race. Measure the time it takes to complete the entire race and divide 30 m by this time to find the actual average speed for this race. How does this speed compare to your predicted average speed?
2. Use your data to estimate how long it would take to walk 100 m. To run 100 m. Test your predictions.
3. Design an experiment to calculate the average speed of someone riding a bicycle. How many m/s do you think a bicycle travels?

EXPLORE

Measuring Motion

In the activity on the previous two pages, you studied several patterns of change of position. You measured the distance each racer moved and how long it took the racer to move that distance. You saw how the times changed when the racer changed his or her method of racing. You then calculated each racer's average speed.

Recall that average speed is equal to the total distance an object travels divided by the total time it takes to travel that distance. This can be written mathematically as follows.

$$\text{average speed} = \frac{\text{total distance}}{\text{total time}}$$

How does a scientist measure speed? A scientist will ask the same two questions you asked, "What distance did an object move? How much time did it take the object to move that distance?" By using these two pieces of information, a scientist calculates an object's average speed the same way you did in your Science Triathlon.

Minds On! How many ways can you tell that a car is moving? The most common way is simply to look at it. If a car is located to the left of you now, and a few seconds later it is located to your right, you know it has moved or you have moved. But do you always need to use your eyes to detect motion?

Imagine you're sitting in a car with a blindfold over your eyes. Could you tell if the car started to move? What would you feel if the car started off very quickly, turned a corner, or came to a sudden stop? Would the sound of the car's engine be different when it started moving? If the car's windows were open, would the air hitting your face feel different when the car started to move? What are all the different ways that you can sense motion?

The average speed of a runner is equal to the total distance run divided by the total time it takes to run that distance.

Long before there were baseball pitchers throwing fastballs or astronomers studying the motions of planets, people wanted to know how things moved. Humans living 100,000 years ago were motion experts. Hunters heaving a rock or a spear at wild game needed an accurate throw to get food.

Today's physicists are just as interested as those early hunters in how things move. **Physicists** (fiz´ ə sists) are scientists who study the structure and interactions of matter, as well as the changes in position that matter undergoes.

Matter is the "stuff" that makes up everything in the universe. Skyscrapers, ants, planets, and pollen grains are all composed of matter. Physicists have found that matter moves in predictable ways.

Physicists often measure the motion of matter, or speed, in meters per second. Everyday measures of speed such as how fast a car or airplane is traveling are given in kilometers per hour in most of the world. (A kilometer is 1,000 meters, about 0.62 mile.) Only one country, the United States, still uses the English units of inch, foot, yard, and mile to measure distance. When using English units, speed is usually given in feet per second or miles per hour.

Travel Agents—Time, Distance, and Direction Experts!

Physicists aren't the only people who need to be motion experts. Travel agents also need to be motion experts.

"What's the best way to make the following trip? I need to fly from Durham, North Carolina, early Wednesday and arrive in Tulsa, Oklahoma, by 11:00 A.M. Wednesday. Then, I need to be in Oklahoma City the next day for a 2:00 P.M. meeting. Should I rent a car at the airport or fly from Tulsa to Oklahoma City?"

Travel agents answer questions like this every day. Their job is to find the fastest, most convenient, and most economical means of travel for people who travel for business or for fun. They must have a knowledge of time, distance, and direction.

Travel agents spend much of their time working with computers. Their computers link them with airline, train, and hotel information networks so they can give their clients several different travel options.

When they're not working on their computers, travel agents may be taking free trips to learn about vacation resorts. They're working during these trips, but they also get to do some sightseeing!

In 1990, the winning Indy race car traveled about 807 kilometers (500 miles) in 2.69 hours.

In 1911, the winning Indy race car traveled about 807 kilometers (500 miles) in 6.67 hours.

Matter in Motion

Scientists investigating an object's motion will also want to know in what direction the object is moving. When both the speed and direction of an object are known, the object's **velocity** (və los' i tē) can be defined.

Physicists are careful to distinguish between speed, which describes how fast an object is moving, and velocity, which describes both speed and direction. Nonscientists often use velocity and speed incorrectly to describe the same motion. For example, a car traveling on a curvy road with its cruise control set at 88 kilometers (about 55 miles) per hour would stay at a constant speed of 88 kilometers per hour. However, this car's velocity would vary, though its speedometer always read the same. The car's velocity changes every time the car changes direction on a curve.

How do you use measures of speed and distance in everyday life? Knowing your speed and the distance you need to travel allows you to estimate how much time it will take to reach a certain destination. Suppose you wanted to travel from Atlanta, Georgia, to Indianapolis, Indiana, to see the famous Indy 500 automobile race. How long would it take to get there in a car traveling at an average speed of 80 kilometers (about 50 miles) per hour?

By checking a map, you learn that Atlanta and Indianapolis are about 800 kilometers (500 miles) apart—the same distance that the Indy 500 cars will go during the race. To calculate the time you would need to allow for travel, you divide the distance you will go by your average speed: 800 kilometers ÷ 80 kilometers per hour = about 10 hours. It would take you a bit more than ten hours of driving to complete this trip even if you did not stop for food and fuel.

How long would it take the winning Indy 500 race cars to travel the same distance, about 800 kilometers, at their top speed? The answer changes every year. Race cars are constantly being redesigned to go faster while maintaining safety. Sometimes bad weather or accidents slow the average speed of the race cars. In 1911, the first year that the Indy 500 was held, the winning car averaged about 120 kilometers (about 75 miles) per hour. In 1990, the winning car averaged 300 kilometers (186 miles) per hour.

Cars like this race about 807 kilometers (500 miles) at the Indy 500 race.

Have you ever stopped at the top of a steep hill, then coasted down on a skateboard or bicycle? Were you going at the same speed at the bottom of the hill as you had been near the top? Describe how your speed changed as you went down the hill.

The moving objects you've studied so far in this unit have all been moving at a constant speed. How can you tell for sure if you're moving at a constant speed or if your speed changes? One way to do this is to measure your change in position (how far you move) during a standard period of time (such as one second). To see how this works, do the Moving Marbles activity.

The girl on the bike is pedaling along at a steady rate on flat ground. Her average speed is three meters per second. If her speed is constant, she'll travel three meters in the first second, another three meters in the next second, another three meters in the following second, and so on until she puts on the brakes to slow down or pedals faster to speed up. An object traveling at **constant speed** moves the same distance during each second of travel.

But what if the girl on the bicycle stops at the top of a steep hill? How will her speed change when she starts down? In the first second, she moves a short distance down the hill. She isn't moving fast—only one meter per second. During the next second, she picks up speed and is moving at two meters per second. If the hill flat-

TRY THIS Activity!

Moving Marbles!

What You Need

2 metersticks, masking tape, 2 school books, stopwatch, marble, *Activity Log* page 5

Tape 2 metersticks together so they form a V-shaped track as shown. Place this track on a long table or desk. Prop the first 10 cm of the track up on 2 school books. Place the marble in the higher end of the track. Let it roll down the track while your partner uses a stopwatch to call out time as it passes— "One second, two seconds," and so on. Note the distance as your partner calls out the time, and record in your ***Activity Log***. Repeat 2 more times. Calculate the distance the marble travels during each of the seconds. Average the distance and record in your ***Activity Log***. Subtract the average distance moved at 1 second from the average distance moved at 2 seconds. Subtract the average distance moved at 2 seconds from the average distance moved at 3 seconds. Record these numbers. Did your marble move the same average distance during each of the seconds?

tened out at this point, she could continue to coast at two meters per second for a while. But since she's on a steep hill, her speed continues to increase. After several more seconds, she's moving at six meters per second. Coasting down a steep hill on a bike is an example of acceleration. Scientists define **acceleration** as the rate of change of an object's velocity.

You saw in the Moving Marbles activity that the marble moved different distances each second. It was accelerating. How might you tell that the girl riding the bike down the hill was accelerating?

You probably think of something speeding up when you hear the term acceleration. This is only partly true. Scientists define all changes in speed or direction as acceleration. An object that is slowing down has negative acceleration. This is why scientists use the term velocity very carefully. Remember, velocity describes both the speed and the direction of a moving object. When an object changes direction, its velocity changes even if its speed does not.

In this lesson, you won't be asked to calculate an object's acceleration. However, it's important for you to be able to answer yes or no to the question, "Is this object accelerating?"

0 m/s

1 m/s 1 m/s

2 m/s 2 m/s

6 m/s   5 m/s   4 m/s 3 m/s   3 m/s 3 m/s 3 m/s 3 m/s

Amazing Motion in the Animal Kingdom

You've learned about motion, speed, velocity, and acceleration of humans. What about the animals on Earth? Animals can reach amazing speeds and achieve rapid acceleration. Here are some maximum speeds of living organisms. How do the maximum speeds of animals compare with the maximum speeds of humans?

Organism/Conditions	Speed (kilometers per hour)
homing pigeon - level flight, no wind	97
hummingbird - level flight	37
hummingbird - power dive	97
African elephant	39
African rhinoceros	48
cheetah	112
greyhound	64
California sea lion - under water	16
Pacific bottlenose porpoise	30
racehorse	76
dragonfly	80
human - running short distance	45
human - running 1.6 kilometers (1 mile)	24
human - swimming	8
human - riding a bicycle	68

Just in Time

Do you sometimes use interesting expressions about how fast things are moving? These expressions often contain comparisons to animals. How slow is "a snail's pace"? How fast does a deer run? The actual speeds of objects used in some expressions like these are given.

Write a funny story that uses all (or most) of these sayings about speed. Feel free to invent your own expressions of speed for the story, too!

Expression	Speed
"slow as a turtle"	0.16 km/h
"quick as a fox"	64 km/h
"move at a snail's pace"	5.0 cm/minute
"faster than a speeding bullet"	275 m/s to 320 m/s
"a blazing fastball"	165 km/h
"a mile a minute"	96.5 km/h
"escape velocity"	40,000 km/h
"runs like a deer"	56 km/h
"like a streak of lightning"	300,000 km/s
"like the speed of sound"	335 m/s

A stopwatch can be used to time the motion of elephants, cheetahs, ostriches, and swimmers.

Sum It Up

In this lesson, you've learned how to determine the speed of an object. When you calculated speed in your Science Triathlon, you divided the distance the racer moved by the time it took him or her to move that distance. You discovered, too, how speed differs from velocity; velocity includes the object's direction of motion. If an object's velocity is changing, then the object is accelerating. Speed, velocity, and acceleration describe the patterns of change of motion by showing various kinds of change in an object's position.

Critical Thinking

1. Why is it called *average* speed?
2. What's the difference between speed and velocity?
3. What's your average speed if it takes you 30 minutes to walk to a friend's house that is two kilometers away?
4. Think about riding in a car from your home to school. How would you determine your average speed? When would the car accelerate?
5. Can speed ever be negative? What about acceleration? If so, give an example.

Theme **T** SYSTEMS and INTERACTIONS

The release of energy from inside Earth caused forces to occur that led to the eruption of Mount St. Helens on May 18, 1980.

What Is Force?

Mount St. Helens before the May 18, 1980 eruption

Every day you experience several different forces, but you may not call them forces. You may say, "This book was pushed across the desk," or "I pulled my brother to school in a wagon." In this lesson, you'll learn about several kinds of forces and what causes them to occur.

Mount St. Helens after the May 18, 1980 eruption

Suddenly, the north side of Mount St. Helens rippled like water. Rocks and ice crashed down the sides of the volcano into the lake below. An enormous blast of scorching gas filled the air with ash traveling faster than the speed of sound. Two geologists flying over the mountain witnessed an amazing release of energy from inside Earth.

This release of energy caused tremendous forces to occur. In a matter of minutes, these forces caused the eruption and landslides that tore off the top 400 meters (about 1,300 feet) of Mount St. Helens. Its snow-covered peak was scarred by a crater 600 meters (about 2,000 feet) deep and 2,100 meters (about 6,900 feet) wide. A deadly blanket of hot, smoking ash soon covered a huge area around the mountain. Ash blocked out the sun in nearby towns, making noon as dark as night. The blast tossed 18-wheel logging trucks into the air, splintered ancient trees, and knocked down whole forests.

Matter is pushed and pulled about by the force of this tornado.

Volcanic eruptions, floods, earthquakes, hurricanes, tornadoes—in all of these spectacular events, matter is pushed and hurled about. These events unleash forces that shape and reshape Earth. Natural disasters are easy to study because they make obvious changes on Earth. However, scientists don't fully understand all the other forces shaping our planet.

Until the 1960s, few scientists had studied the enormous forces that occur within Earth that form mountains, move continents, and produce ocean basins. These forces are hard to study because the changes they cause occur deep underground over a very long period of time.

The landmasses we call continents don't appear to be moving, but they are. Geologists, scientists who study the structure of Earth, have discovered that continents and oceans float like rafts on top of 15 huge plates of rock that cover Earth's surface. Plates can move from one to ten centimeters per year, carrying entire continents or ocean basins with them. The forces required to move these plates are enormous. Scientists are still investigating how these forces are produced.

Where different plates collide, mountains are pushed up, volcanoes form, and earthquakes occur. Old areas of Earth's surface are sometimes buried deep under other plates, and new land forms in rifts or cracks between the plates. The eruptions of Mount St. Helens and the volcanic mountains in the northwestern United States are examples of what happens in an area where two plates are colliding.

Of course, not every force in the world is strong enough to move mountains. To feel different strengths of forces, do the Try This Activity on the next page.

When two plates collide, one plate can slide under the other. Part of the plate material moves down and melts. This melted material rises and when it reaches the surface, it produces a volcano.

Plates are blocks of Earth's crust and upper mantle.

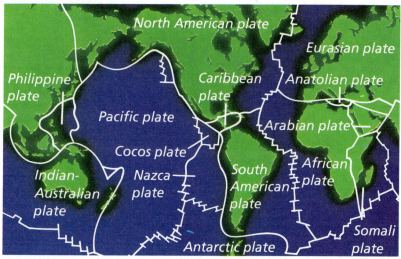

Activity!
TRY THIS

Experience a Force

Now you can experience a force.

What You Need
your hands, hand lotion, *Activity Log* page 6

Place your hands together lightly. Rub your hands back and forth quickly. Is it hard to move them this way? How do they feel when you stop?

Press your hands together tightly. Rub them back and forth. How do they feel when you stop?

Apply hand lotion to your hands. Press your hands together tightly and rub them back and forth. Write your observations in your *Activity Log*.

EXPLORE Activity!

Slipping and Sliding

In this activity, you'll pull an object across a table to see if changing the surface between the object and the table changes the force needed to move it across the table.

What You Need

smooth, level desk or table
3 small school books (all the same size)
2 self-sealing plastic food bags
2-m length of string
2 pencils
roller skate (optional)
sheet of sandpaper (at least as wide as the book covers)
masking tape
Activity Log pages 7–8

What To Do

1. Place 2 books in 1 bag and 1 book in the other bag. Seal the bags. Place both bags on a smooth table and tie the string around them. Leave 1 m of string between the bags. Move the bags until the string between them is tight and the bag containing 1 book is hanging off the edge of the table.

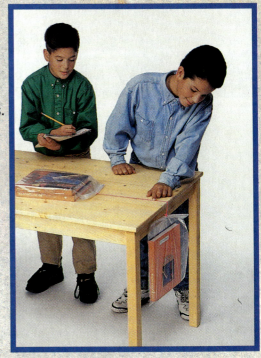

2 Let go of the bag hanging off the table. Record your observations in your *Activity Log*. Repeat this step 2 more times. What do you observe?

3 Tape a sheet of sandpaper onto the table, rough side up. Place the bag containing 2 books on top of it and let the bag containing 1 book hang off the table. Release the bag hanging off the table. Record your observation in your *Activity Log*. Repeat this step 2 more times.

4 What would happen if the books were sliding across the table on rollers? Write your prediction in your *Activity Log*. Place 2 pencils underneath the bag holding the 2 books. Let the bag holding 1 book pull them across the table. Record your observation in your *Activity Log*.

What Happened?

1. What supplied the force to slide the books across the table?
2. What had to happen for the books to slide across the table?
3. In what ways do the books slide differently if you set them on sandpaper? On pencils? Why do you think this is the case?
4. Are any forces affecting the sliding books besides the pull of the book?

What Now?

1. Can you think of other ways to make it easier to slide the books across the table? What would happen if you put them on a small cart or a roller skate? Test one of your ideas.
2. Can you think of a toy or a game that uses a sliding object? Describe the game. Could you still play the game if the sliding object were coated with rubber cement? Coated with oil?

What Can We Find Out About Forces?

A **force** is a push or a pull that one object exerts on another object. It takes a force to start a lump of matter moving, stop it from moving, or change its velocity.

Friction is a force that opposes motion between the surfaces of two objects that are touching. Friction depends on the kinds of surfaces between the two objects and on the amount of force pressing the two objects together. Friction causes moving objects to slow down and eventually stop. It always acts in the direction opposite to the movement of an object.

Friction also occurs between two touching objects that are just sitting still. In this case, the frictional force between the two objects is just great enough and in the right direction to balance out any other forces that are acting on the objects at that time. The total force on the two objects is zero, and the objects won't start to move.

The more friction that exists between the bow and the violin strings, the easier it is to set the strings in motion.

There's no acceleration. The more force pressing two objects together, the more friction there is between those two objects.

You've done two activities that demonstrated how friction affects moving objects. When you rubbed your hands together hard in the activity on page 27, you felt your palms get hot. Friction produces heat. In the Explore Activity, you found it's harder to pull a book across a piece of sandpaper than across a smooth table. The rough surface of the sandpaper increased the friction between the book and the table. The book moved more slowly across the sandpaper than across the smooth table. These activities demonstrated two of the main effects of friction: warming up moving surfaces and slowing down moving objects. Now do the following activity to use friction to make music.

TRY THIS Activity!

Friction Music

Ben Franklin made music with friction. You can try his experiment.

What You Need
drinking glass with stem (half full of water), lemon juice, *Activity Log* page 9

Make sure the glass you use has no dents or chips on the rim. Hold the glass firmly on the table with one hand. Wet one of the fingers of your other hand and rub it around the rim of the glass in a circular motion. As you rub around the rim, press on it very gently at first. Slowly increase the pressure until the glass produces a clear, bell-like tone. **Safety Tip:** Hold the glass steady, and don't press so hard that you break it!

If you have trouble making the glass ring, wash your hands with soap and rinse them with water to remove any soap film. Dipping the tips of your fingers in a few drops of lemon juice will also help to increase the force of friction between your fingers and the rim of the glass.

After you can make the glass ring, change the amount of water. Does the sound change when you raise or lower the water level? Can you change the sound by rubbing faster or slower? By pressing harder or softer? Can you and your class play a tune? Record your answers in your *Activity Log*.

Friction Can Make Beautiful Music

Sounds produced by the friction of two objects rubbing together can be irritating or pleasing. Squeaking chalk across a blackboard makes people cringe. Crickets attract their mates by rubbing their front wings together to make chirping sounds. But rubbing a bow across the strings of a violin or strumming a guitar string can start the strings vibrating and make music.

The quality and amount of sound produced when two objects rub together partly depends on the amount of friction between them. Recall that when you dipped your fingers in lemon juice you increased the friction between your fingers and the glass. Bows for stringed instruments are made by attaching hairs from the tail of a horse to a wooden bow. Horsehairs are smooth. Violinists rub rosin on the hairs of their bow to increase the friction between the bow and the strings. The more friction there is between the bow and the strings, the easier it is to set the strings in motion when the bow slides across them. The vibrations of the violin's strings make the musical sounds you hear.

In 1763 Benjamin Franklin invented an instrument called the glass harmonica. It consisted of glass bowls mounted on a spindle that was turned by a foot pedal. By moving his fingers from one bowl to the next, he could play complete musical pieces.

Friction and the Environment

Reducing friction is good for the environment and good for your wallet.

Improperly inflated tire.

Properly inflated tire.

What would you do if you learned a simple way to reduce friction that would cost you nothing, would help decrease air pollution, and could save money? Would you be willing to try it?

All you need to do is to get the automobile owners you know to inflate the tires on their cars to the maximum safe pressure recommended.

Badly underinflated tires produce more friction and increase the amount of gasoline a car burns by as much as six percent.

In the United States, manufacturers are required by law to produce cars that get an average of 44 kilometers (about 28 miles) per gallon of gasoline. Since most people drive their cars about 24,000 kilometers (about 15,000 miles) per year, car owners buy about 2,070 liters (about 545 gallons) of gas a year at a cost of about $818.

Underinflated tires produce more friction than properly inflated tires and make it harder for the car to move along the road. When tires are underinflated, they wobble from side to side. This increases the friction between the road and the tire. The extra friction will cause fuel mileage to drop to 41 kilometers (about 26 miles) per gallon. This may not sound like a big change, but it means that the driver will have to spend about $52 per year more to drive the same distance. Because the car is burning more gasoline, it will also put an additional 665 pounds of CO_2 (carbon dioxide) into the atmosphere. CO_2 is one of the "greenhouse gases" that scientists are studying to see if they produce long-term changes in Earth's climate.

What forces are involved in a karate kick and punch?

Minds On! What is giving a push or a pull in these pictures? Forces are acting in every case. How many pushes and pulls can you identify for each of the pictures?

What forces are involved in a golf swing?

What forces are involved when a child on a swing drags both feet on the ground?

The diver is falling toward the water because of the force of gravity.

Forces in Your World

You need to know two things to determine the effect of a force on an object—the direction of the force (which way it's pushing or pulling) and how strong the force is (its magnitude).

Why does a diver jumping off a ten-meter platform fall toward the water? To answer, you need to know all the forces acting on the diver. What's the direction of the force? How strong is it? Are there any other forces acting at the same time?

One force you'll need to consider is gravity. Gravity is the force that pulls us toward the ground and holds water in the bathtub. Gravitational forces hold the moon in orbit around Earth and hold the planets in orbits around the sun.

The diver falls toward the water because gravity is a force acting between her and the water and because there is no longer a force pushing up on the diver, as there was when she was standing on the diving platform. **Gravity** is a pulling force that every object exerts on every other object. The force of gravity depends on the masses of the objects and the distance between them. More massive objects result in a greater gravitational force. Since Earth is so much more massive than the diver, the movement of Earth "up" toward the diver is not noticeable. You observe the diver falling. The pull of gravity exists between all objects. Unless very massive, however, the pull between them is not very large. You don't notice any pull between you and your friend, even when you stand very close together. But because Earth is very massive, the pull between you and Earth is easy to detect. It is this force that is always pulling us and all other objects toward the ground.

As the distance between two objects

decreases, the pull of gravity between them increases. As the distance increases, the pull of gravity decreases.

You've probably been asked how much you weigh. You most likely answered in pounds. You may recall that scientists define weight as the force of gravity acting on a mass on Earth's surface. The unit of force used by scientists is the newton, and the symbol for newton is N. Weight is a measure of force, so it's expressed as newtons.

You need a measuring device to tell how strong a force is. Scientists often use spring scales to measure the magnitude of a force. A medium-sized apple hanging in a tree pulls down on the tree limb with a force of about one newton. The diver shown is being pulled downward by gravity with a force equal to her weight in newtons.

Scientists have tested the strength of Earth's gravity and found it to be just about the same all over the world. So anywhere on our planet that the diver performs, Earth's gravity will pull her down with about the same magnitude of force. But gravity will pull a person of greater mass with a greater pull.

Identifying the direction and strength of gravity, the main force acting on the diver, is easy. But answering the physicist's last question— "Are any other forces acting?"—is trickier. There are always several forces acting on all matter in motion near the surface of Earth. Many are hard to notice. However, one force always should be accounted for—the force of friction.

There's friction between the diver and the air. The diver's body pushes the air out of the way as she falls toward the water. This type of friction is called air resistance or drag. Do the Try This Activity to discover some properties of air resistance.

TRY THIS Activity!

Air Resistance

You can feel friction between the air and an object.

What You Need
1 large piece of stiff cardboard
Activity Log **page 10**

Stand in a clear area and hold the piece of cardboard away from you. Swing it through the air. Did you feel the resistance of the air against the cardboard?

Design another experiment with the cardboard to feel the force of air resistance. You may wish to cut or fold it. Write directions for your new experiment and the results you get in your ***Activity Log.***

Air resistance isn't a strong force for divers leaping from a ten-meter platform. Most divers never notice friction between themselves and the air. Astronauts, however, are especially interested in friction between the skin of their spacecraft and Earth's atmosphere.

Friction heats the skin of satellites reentering the atmosphere to several thousand degrees. Spacecraft returning to Earth must have heat shields. Otherwise, the heat generated by friction with the air would damage or destroy the spacecraft and its contents.

Heat-resistant tiles cover the fuselage of this spacecraft. These tiles shield the spacecraft from the heat generated by friction as the spacecraft reenters Earth's atmosphere.

Dynamic Diving on the Moon

If astronauts someday build a swimming pool on the moon, a diver could do much fancier dives than are possible here on Earth! On the moon, divers would fall ten meters from the platform to the water much more slowly than on Earth. With more time before hitting the water, spectacular dives would be easy! How is this possible?

Gravity exerts about the same amount of force everywhere on Earth's surface, but other places in the universe have different amounts of gravity. On the moon, the force of gravity is only one-sixth as strong as on Earth. The force of gravity is proportional to the mass of the objects. Earth is about six times more massive than the moon. Since the pull of the moon's gravity is weaker than the pull of Earth's gravity, falling objects accelerate toward the moon's surface more slowly than they would on Earth. The moon doesn't have an atmosphere, so air resistance wouldn't be a problem, either.

Can you think of other amazing feats you could do on the moon? Can you think of things that might be harder or more awkward to do on the moon? **1**

Do You Have To Be Touching To Push or Pull?

You touch directly most of the things that push and pull you around. When you shove a refrigerator or zoom off on roller skates, you have a physical link to the thing you are pulling or pushing. You know gravity is a force that works without touching. Is it possible to exert another type of force without touching something? The Moving Magnets activity below will help you discover an answer.

This train floats above the track due to the magnetic force from the train and the magnetic force from the track. The train "floats" because these magnetic forces push each other away. Is there a lot of friction between the train and the track?

TRY THIS Activity!

Moving Magnets

What You Need
3 ring magnets, wooden pencil, *Activity Log* page 11

Stick the pencil through the hole in one of the magnets. Hold the pencil so the sharp end is pointing toward the ceiling. Place another magnet on the point of the pencil, and slowly lower it toward the bottom of the pencil. Are the magnets exerting a force on each other? Describe the force you feel. Remove the top magnet, but don't take the bottom magnet off the pencil. Turn the top magnet over and put it back on the pencil so its opposite side faces the bottom magnet. Slowly lower the top magnet as before. Do the magnets exert a force on each other this time? Is it the same kind of force you felt before? Describe the differences in the forces you feel in your *Activity Log*. Can magnets exert a force when they aren't touching each other? How can you tell? Can magnets exert both a push and a pull? What determines whether magnets push apart or pull together? Experiment by putting 3 magnets on the same pencil in different ways. Can you make 2 magnets "float" above the bottom magnet? Sketch the positions of the magnets when they are floating or sticking together. Are there similarities or differences between the magnetic forces and the force of gravity?

Friction Forces: Design and Engineering Aspects

Friction makes things hard to move. Transportation engineers and designers develop oils and lubricants to reduce friction in car engines and other moving parts. They also use wind tunnels to test the friction between high-speed air and car bodies. Streamlined vehicles slip through the air with less friction, so they use less gasoline and therefore cause less air pollution.

Transportation engineers and designers also do research on ways to increase friction! The force produced by the engine of a car couldn't push the car down the road without some friction between the tires and the road. Drivers find that they need more friction when they try to climb a steep hill on ice or stop quickly on badly worn tires. Think of what happens when you try to walk fast or run on ice.

Engineers test new car designs in wind tunnels to determine the amount of air resistance between the car and the air.

Literature Link

Moving Heavy Things

"The cunning ways friction has been reduced would please the great Leonardo da Vinci. Monument builders move marble, granite, and slate blocks on their bases with ice cubes, adjusting positions and then allowing the unwieldy weights to melt into place. Sheet metal workers move half-ton flats of sheet copper and stainless steel by levering them up and rolling baseballs beneath them."
(excerpted from *Moving Heavy Things* by Jan Adkins)

What heavy things might you want to move more easily by reducing friction? Think of a very heavy thing, and draw a way to move it that reduces friction to a minimum. Show your drawing to a classmate. Have him or her write a sentence telling what's happening in your drawing.

Ancient Egyptian sleds, modern dog sleds, and modern snowmobiles all use runners to reduce the friction between the sled and the ground.

GLOBAL PERSPECTIVE

The Evolution of Sleds

The first vehicle designed by humans wasn't a cart with wheels, but a sled. About 10,000 years ago, people built sleds consisting of platforms with runners.

Sleds allowed people to drag heavier loads than they could carry. Egyptians used sleds to move giant stones for the pyramids. They sometimes greased the runners for easier sliding. What force were they trying to reduce?

The Inuit (in' ü it) people are Native Americans who live in snow-covered northern Alaska and Canada. They transport heavy loads such as the bodies of seals, whales, and other wildlife to their villages.

Inuit designers over 1,000 years ago designed an efficient sled that could be pulled by dog teams. It's lightweight, has low-friction runners, and can carry heavy loads over snow and ice. The basic design is still in use. One thing has changed, however. Snowmobiles, rather than dogs, provide the force to pull many Inuit sleds today!

Sum It Up

In this lesson, you've learned that forces push and pull matter and that motion occurs only if the position of an object is changed. Friction acts to oppose motion and causes objects to slow down or stop. Another familiar force is gravity. Objects exert gravitational force on all other objects. The strength of the force of gravity between any two objects depends on their masses and the distance between them. Friction, gravity, and other forces interact and are important considerations for transportation designers and engineers, who work on new means of moving matter from one place to another.

Critical Thinking

1. What is friction? Is the force of friction greater between two children on a sled and the snow or between only one of the children on the same sled and the snow? Why?
2. Would it be possible to walk if there were no friction? Explain.
3. What forces are acting on a ball just after it is thrown?
4. Explain why astronauts weigh less on the moon.
5. Why is the pull of gravity on the moon less than the pull of gravity on Earth?

39

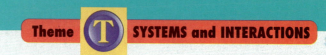

Can an Object Start or Stop Moving Without Help From a Force?

Starting and stopping, slowing down and speeding up–you probably experience these actions every day. Do you ever wonder what causes an object to start or stop moving? What might happen if people couldn't start or stop moving when they needed to? In this lesson, you'll find out how objects at rest can be made to move and how objects in motion can be made to stop.

Wildfire gallops onto the racecourse carrying her jockey. They are competing in a steeplechase—a contest of fence-jumping and speed. The horse and jockey who clear all the fences in the shortest time will become champions.

Wildfire approaches the first barrier—a fence 1.5 meters (about 5 feet) tall. The jockey gives a slight nudge to the horse's side. The horse springs forward, jumping the fence with room to spare. They make a slight turn and line up for the next hurdle.

Wildfire changes her stride as horse and jockey approach the next barrier, a wall with two rails on top. The horse is a little off balance and senses she cannot make a clean jump. Will she hit the rail and fall?

The jockey urges her to hurdle the wall, but Wildfire refuses. At the last possible moment she drops her head, braces her front legs, and stops short of the wall, uninjured.

But her jockey does not stop. He keeps moving straight toward the barrier, flies over Wildfire's lowered head, and sails over the wall alone. Gravity pulls the jockey toward Earth's center, and he lands with a thump. Luckily, he's not badly hurt, but he and Wildfire won't win today's race.

Spills like these often happen during steeplechases. Why do objects keep going forward when the platforms they are riding on stop? Do the activity on the right to experience this.

You've just read about a jockey clearing the fence even when the horse stopped, and you've observed the motions of water balloons after they left your hand when you stopped running. How are these situations similar?

Both the jockey and the water balloons were riding on a moving platform (the horse and your hand). Both platforms were moving forward in a straight line. The horse was galloping toward the fence and you were running toward the finish line. Each of the platforms suddenly stopped. What happened to the motion of the jockey and the balloons?

If the horse stops moving, what happens to the jockey?

TRY THIS Activity!

Moving Balloons

You'll use balloons to test motion. What can you discover?

What You Need

masking tape, meterstick, 2 balloons, water, *Activity Log* page 12

Mark a "start" and "finish" line with masking tape on the pavement 10 m apart. Tape a "warning" line 1 m in front of the finish line. Fill the balloon with water and tie a knot in the open end. Hold it by the knotted end out to the side of your body at shoulder height. At the start line, begin to run toward the finish line at a constant speed. Let go of the balloon directly over the warning line. Where did the balloon hit the ground?

Get another water-filled balloon. Set the balloon in the palm of your hand. Go to the start line, raise the balloon away from your body to shoulder height and run down the course again. This time, stop suddenly just as you reach the warning line. What happens to the motion of the balloon? Record your observations in your *Activity Log*.

41

EXPLORE Activity!

Jet Racing Cars

You've seen that if matter is moving, it tends to keep on moving—like the jockey and the water balloons. If matter isn't moving, it will tend to stay where it is—at rest. How can you make matter that is at rest start moving?

What You Need

balloon-powered jet car
4 nickels
meterstick
lightweight cardboard
   8 1/2" x 11"
masking tape
scissors
Activity Log pages 13–14

What To Do

1. Make a balloon inflation gauge by cutting the sheet of cardboard into a "U" shape. The opening of the "U" should be 12 cm wide.

2. Mark a starting line by sticking the masking tape on a smooth, level floor or table surface 2 m long. Place the meterstick so that one end is even with the starting line.

3. Have one person blow up the balloon until it just fits into the opening of the inflation gauge. Have the same person blow up the balloon every time, and use the inflation gauge so there will be the same amount of air inside.

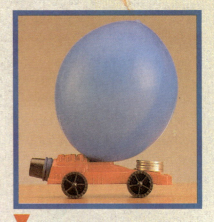

4. Assemble the balloon and car as shown in the diagram. Set the car on the starting line and let the air rush out of the balloon. Record your observations of how far the car traveled in your *Activity Log*. Repeat 3 more times and calculate the average distance in your *Activity Log*.

5. Use a piece of tape to attach a nickel to the top of the jet car. Repeat steps 3 and 4. Does it go as far or as fast? How does the average distance compare with your first trial?

6. Tape another nickel to the car. Repeat steps 3 and 4.

7. Now test the car 4 times with a load of 3 nickels, then 4 times with 4 nickels. Measure the distances the car travels, calculate the average distances, and record them in your **Activity Log**.

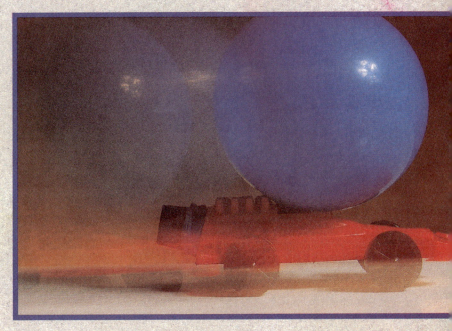

What causes this jet car to accelerate?

What Happened?

1. Which accelerated faster—the jet car carrying 4 nickels or the jet car with no extra mass placed on it? Which of these had the greater average distance?
2. Why is it important to use the inflation gauge every time to be sure you blow up the balloon to the same size?

What Now?

1. Would it be possible to get the jet car carrying 4 nickels to accelerate as fast as the jet car that has no extra mass placed on it? How could you do that? Design a new balloon inflation gauge to try this.
2. Two identical pickup trucks are entered in a drag race. The trucks' engines, tires, and bodies are exactly the same, but one of them is carrying a load of bricks in the back. Which truck will probably win the race? Why?

EXPLORE

Why Does Matter Sit Still? Why Does Matter Keep Moving?

A net force must be applied to both the pebble and the boulder to start them moving.

To answer these questions, let's review your readings and explorations so far. Recall the steeplechase contest and the water balloon race. The motion of the jockey and the motion of water balloons demonstrated a basic property of all matter: Moving matter tends to keep moving in a straight line and at a constant speed unless acted upon by a net force. But what about matter that isn't moving? Is a big lump of matter that is sitting on the ground and not moving (like the big boulder shown in the picture) likely to start moving all by itself? What about a much smaller lump of matter, like the pebble in the girl's hand?

The answer to both questions is no! Matter tends to keep doing what it's already doing. This is true whether the lump is big (like the boulder) or small (like the pebble).

How Is It Possible to Move Matter?

To start matter moving, a net force must be applied to it. Recall from Lesson 2 that a force is a push or a pull that one object exerts on another object. What is a net force? You can experience a net force by doing the Pulling Forces activity below.

Activity!

Pulling Forces

You'll be able to demonstrate a net force using washers in this activity.

What You Need
metal washer, 2 rubber bands, 2 newton spring scales, pencil, paper, goggles, *Activity Log* page 15

Work with a partner. Tie each rubber band to opposite sides of the washer. Attach the spring scales to the free ends of the rubber bands. Place your setup on a sheet of paper on a flat surface. Trace around the washer.

Each person should pull on a spring scale at the same time in opposite directions with the same amount of force (the same number of newtons). **Safety Tip:** Do not pull too hard. Record your observations in your *Activity Log*.

Now each person should pull on a spring scale with a different amount of force, but still in opposite directions. Record your observations in your *Activity Log*.

Balanced forces are equal in size but opposite in direction. When you pulled on the washer the first time, the forces you exerted on it were balanced. The washer won't move from its original position when the forces acting on it are balanced forces.

But what if forces are unbalanced? Unbalanced forces can occur when one force is larger than the other. Unbalanced forces can also occur when one force is not directly opposite the other force. When you pulled on the washer the second time, the forces you exerted on it were unbalanced, and the washer moved.

What will happen if you pull on the washer with equal forces that aren't in opposite directions? Try it.

A **net force** on an object exists when the forces acting on it are unbalanced. A net force will cause an object to start moving, speed up, slow down, stop moving, or change direction. Another way of saying this is that a net force will cause a change in the position of an object or a change in the velocity of an object. Recall that velocity describes both the speed and direction of an object.

Think back to the very beginning of this unit. Remember the tug-of-war contests. In which pictures on pages 8 and 9 do unbalanced forces exist?

Why Are Some Objects Harder To Move or Harder To Stop Than Others?

Look back at the pictures of the boulder and the pebble in the girl's hand on page 44. Would it be as easy for you to move the giant boulder as it is for the girl to throw the pebble? Why? The pebble and the boulder are both rocks. Can one rock be much harder to move than another? Why are bricks and barbells more resistant to being moved than cotton balls and bananas?

The two dogs pulling on the shoes are pulling with equal and opposite forces. These are balanced forces.

The two dogs pulling on the rope are pulling with unequal but opposite forces. These are unbalanced forces.

Minds On! Let's look at some rules about matter. One example of each rule is given. Work in groups of three to come up with two or three more examples of each rule. List these examples in one person's *Activity Log* page 16, and have all three group members sign the group's work.

1. Moving matter tends to keep moving in a straight line and at a constant speed. (When a horse stops suddenly, its jockey still moves forward.)
2. Matter at rest tends to stay at rest. (Rocks don't move without a push or pull by something.)
3. An unbalanced force or a net force is required to change the speed or direction of moving matter. (Air streaming out of the balloon caused the jet car to move forward. The forces on the jet car were then unbalanced and the jet car began to accelerate.)
4. The more matter an object contains (the more mass it has), the harder it is to change its speed or direction of motion. (A jet car carrying four nickels hardly moves when the balloon's air is released.)

In 1686, Sir Isaac Newton combined these different rules about how matter moves into a single statement we now call Newton's First Law of Motion. The First Law of Motion is—

> **An object at rest tends to stay at rest and an object in motion tends to stay in motion in a straight line and at a constant speed, unless acted upon by a net force.**

Newton's statement of the First Law of Motion is also known as the Law of Inertia. **Inertia** (in ûr´ shə) is the property of matter that resists changes in speed or direction of motion. The more mass an object possesses, the more inertia that object possesses, therefore the larger the net force that will be needed to change its velocity. Remember that velocity includes both speed and direction. A change in velocity can be an increase or a decrease.

Inertia is a basic property of all kinds of matter. From the smallest subatomic particle to the largest galaxy, every speck of matter possesses mass and therefore possesses inertia. The amount of mass each object possesses is a measure of that object's inertia.

In the Jet Racing Cars activity, you saw how more massive objects (the jet car with mass added) had more inertia and did not accelerate (change velocity) as much as the less massive object (the jet car without mass added) did when the same amount of net force was applied. You would have needed to apply a larger net force to the jet car with more mass added to get it to accelerate as much as the jet car with no mass added.

Is this man carrying real boulders or fake boulders?

What Controls How Much Inertia There Is in Matter?

The amount of inertia present in a lump of matter depends partly on size. If you have two barbells made of exactly the same kind of metal, the bigger barbell will have more inertia and be harder to lift.

However, size alone doesn't determine an object's inertia. Look at the picture of the boulder being used in a movie. It looks as if it should have a large amount of inertia and would therefore be very hard to pick up (change its velocity). You've probably already figured out how the man is able to move what you see in the picture with very little force—the boulder is a fake. It's made out of papier-mâché, not granite, as it appears.

The trick boulder shows another important fact about inertia: the amount of inertia that an object possesses depends on both the material the object is made of and the size of the object.

A baseball has more mass than a foam ball of the same diameter; a steel ball the size of a baseball has more mass than both balls. The sizes of the foam ball, baseball, and steel ball are all the same. Their masses are different because the steel ball has more matter in it than the baseball or the foam ball.

Minds On! Have you ever picked up an empty foam ice chest? Only a small amount of net force is needed to change a foam box's velocity from zero (when it is on the ground) to several meters per second.

However, if you fill an empty foam ice chest to the top with ice and soft drinks, it becomes harder to pick up. What will you need to do to pick up a full ice chest? Discuss your answer with your neighbor. •

Sir Isaac Newton developed his ideas about inertia and the laws of motion over a period of years. Read the following pages to learn more about Isaac Newton's work and the way our scientific knowledge changes and is made known.

47

Sir Isaac Newton

Mo-Tzu

Aristotle

Social Studies Link
Scientific Development

Have you ever put off writing a report for school until you were forced to do it? That's what Sir Isaac Newton did with his discoveries of the Laws of Motion and the theory of gravitation. Newton completed his research in 1665 when he was only 23 years old. He didn't write a final draft of his findings for 20 years! *Principia Mathematica*, a book describing Newton's findings, wasn't published until 1687!

Newton's work might have been lost had it not been for his astronomer friend, Edmund Halley. Realizing how important Newton's research on motion would be to other scientists, Halley nagged Newton to rewrite his 20-year-old notes. Halley was so intent on having the book published that he paid the printing costs himself.

After Newton's work was published, scientists did experiments to test his conclusions. Their experimental results supported Newton's observations. Older ideas about motion were rejected in view of Newton's findings.

Aristotle's views on motion had been taught in European universities for almost 2,000 years, but his ideas were disproved in light of Newton's findings. Experimental evidence overturned centuries of reliance on the authority of the Greek philosopher. Aristotle believed that a rock thrown horizontally continued moving because air streamed in behind it and forced the rock forward. Scientists testing Aristotle's statement found no evidence of a forward force. Newton's first law, "an object at rest tends to stay at rest and an object in motion tends to stay in motion in a straight line and at a constant speed, unless acted upon by an outside force," replaced Aristotle's thoughts on motion.

But what if Isaac Newton had not published his discoveries? It's quite possible that you would be studying the law of inertia of Mo-Tzu (mô´ tsü´) as well as the law of gravitation of

Principia Mathematica described Isaac Newton's scientific discoveries.

Scientists are commonly judged both by the quality of their own discoveries and by how those discoveries are used by later generations of scientists. Mo-Tzu is not well-known. Neither is Abu 'l Fath Al-Khazini, an Arabian scientist who stated a law of gravitation 500 years before Newton lived. Their discoveries in physics could have been the starting point for further research but were not, because they weren't published worldwide. That is our loss. Think of how far our knowledge of physics might have advanced by now if the Law of Inertia had been widely known 2,000 years before it was!

Abu 'l Fath Al-Khazini (ä´bü l fäth äl kä zē´ nē). Chinese philosopher Mo-Tzu wrote in the book *Mo Ching:* "The cessation of motion is due to the opposing force...If there is no opposing force...the motion will never stop. This is as true as that an ox is not a horse." This is another way of stating Newton's first law. It was published about 2,000 years before Newton was born.

An 18th century physics book showed this demonstration of Newton's third law of motion.

Lacking any hint that these discoveries had already been made, Sir Isaac Newton rediscovered the Law of Inertia and revolutionized the science of physics. His work laid the groundwork for the discoveries Albert Einstein made at the beginning of the 20th century. But if Edmund Halley hadn't encouraged him to write up his results, Newton probably wouldn't have received credit for his great scientific insights, any more than Abu 'l Fath Al-Khazini and Mo-Tzu did. What's more, we might still be waiting for someone else to rediscover these physical principles—someone who would find support from a large group of other scientists ready to cooperate in understanding them and furthering the scientific insight they provided. A scientific discovery can be thought of as a lighted candle—if a candle is lighted but no one is using its light to look at something, then the light is being wasted.

Potential and Kinetic Energy

An avalanche is the rapid, sudden fall down a mountain slope of ice, snow, rocks, or mud. Avalanches can be deadly to unlucky skiers. Skiers can start an avalanche by moving across a ledge of snow and applying enough force to crack the layers of snow loose. The resulting avalanche may break trees in half, toss cars off roads, and crush houses.

The ice and snow of an avalanche are pulled down the side of a mountain by the force of gravity. Deep layers of snow and ice that build up on mountains possess a large amount of mass. This mass exerts a huge amount of force on whatever it strikes on its way down the mountain. Avalanches may travel only 20 or 30 meters, or they may roll over mountainsides for more than 2,000 meters (more than a mile).

The snow on this mountain has a great deal of potential energy.

This avalanche has a lot of kinetic energy.

Scientists have a way of describing how much force is being exerted and predicting how much damage that force can do when snow is moving down the mountain. If scientists can estimate the mass and velocity of the snow present in an avalanche, they can calculate its kinetic energy. Kinetic energy is energy of motion. **Kinetic (ki net' ik) energy** is the energy an object has because of its motion. An avalanche of a massive snowpack moving very fast down a steep slope will have a large amount of kinetic energy. The more kinetic energy the avalanche has, the more damage the avalanche can do.

As this mass of snow begins to move downhill, its kinetic energy increases.

But geologists want to predict how much damage an avalanche might do before it happens. They can do this by calculating the potential energy of a snowpack. **Potential energy** is energy that an object has due to its position or condition. For example, a stretched rubber band has potential energy because of its condition.

The amount of gravitational potential energy stored in an object depends on two factors: how much mass the object possesses and how high above Earth it is positioned. A massive, icy layer high on a mountainside has more potential energy than a light, snowy layer on a gentle hillside. The more potential energy the ice has, the more damage it can do if it starts to move.

Geologists and other earth scientists study potential avalanche areas each season. They measure the height of the layer of snow and ice on steep slopes, and they calculate its mass. They can then calculate the potential energy of a snow and ice pack in an avalanche-prone area.

On the basis of their measurements and calculations, earth scientists sometimes deliberately start small avalanches before big, dangerous ones can occur. They do this by setting off explosives where there is danger of a big avalanche.

A well-planned explosion will exert just enough force to break loose the ice crystals that hold the pack of snow and ice in place. In other words, the force of the explosion causes matter at rest (the snowpack) to begin to move. This matter has a great amount of inertia. The net force from the explosion must be enough to weaken the frictional forces holding the snowpack in place. Then the snow starts to slide downward because of the force of gravity. The moving snow exerts force as it travels down the slope. Another way of saying this is that the potential energy contained by the snow, while it was at rest on top of the mountain, is converted to kinetic energy as it slides downhill during the avalanche.

How Does the First Law of Motion Apply?

This child will continue to move along the water slide until the force of friction slows him down.

You run up to the water slide, leap forward, and slide ten meters across the lawn on your stomach. It's a great way to spend a hot afternoon! You're taking advantage of the First Law of Motion: moving objects continue moving in a straight line and at a constant speed unless acted upon by some unbalanced force. The unbalanced force of friction between your stomach and the water slide will slow you down gently and bring you to a stop.

Coming gently to a stop instead of continuing to move in a straight line can be a matter of life and death at other times. About 40,000 people in the United States die each year in automobile crashes. When a car moving 80 kilometers (about 50 miles) per hour hits a tree, the car crumples and stops moving, but the floor of the car where the seats are attached doesn't stop as quickly as the front bumper. If the passengers are not wearing seat belts, they'll continue to move forward at the same speed, just as the First Law of Motion predicts. They'll stop very suddenly (like the front bumper) when they crash into the dashboard or windshield.

The passengers will come to a less sudden stop if they're wearing seat belts. Seat belts and air bags save lives by applying an unbalanced force to passengers during the time the car crumples, stopping them from continuing in straight-line motion. By holding them in their seats, the seat belts stop the passengers from crashing through the windshield headfirst. Race car drivers using specially designed seat belt systems often walk away unhurt from crashes that occur at over 320 kilometers (about 200 miles) per hour.

Air bags safely prevent drivers and passengers from continuing to move forward at a constant speed in a straight line toward the windshield.

Safer Cars

Air bags and antilock brakes are two new inventions that help drivers and passengers avoid serious injury and death in car crashes. Both of these devices make cars safer by helping to avoid the problems caused by the fact that objects in motion (cars and passengers) tend to travel in a straight line unless acted upon by an outside force. In other words, air bags and antilock braking systems help you deal safely with Newton's First Law of Motion. Here's how they work. An air bag is a large fabric balloon stored inside the steering column or dashboard of a car. It's connected to collision sensors built into the front of the car and in the passenger compartment. When the sensors detect a change in motion of the car equivalent to the car hitting a brick wall at about 20 kilometers (12 miles) per hour, the sensors send a signal to the air bag. (This speed is about as fast as you can run.) The bag then inflates with nitrogen gas to protect the driver's and the passenger's heads and chests.

An air bag can be used only once. It inflates in less than 50 milliseconds—about half the time it takes you to blink an eye. It cushions your head and chest and prevents you from hitting any hard surface inside the car. In less than one second after impact, the bag starts to deflate. If it has prevented a car occupant from continuing in straight-line motion (as Newton predicted) and slamming face first into the windshield during an accident, it was a good investment in safety.

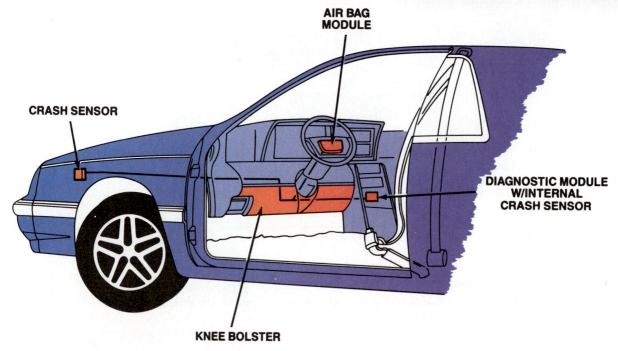

When the crash sensors detect a large decrease in motion, they send a signal to the air bag to inflate.

Antilock braking systems (ABS) are designed to help drivers avoid having an accident by preventing the car from skidding. Many accidents occur when cars go out of control on wet or icy pavement. If the driver pushes down on the brake pedal too hard in a car with standard brakes, the wheels stop turning and the tires begin to skid.

When a tire is skidding, it can't apply enough force to the road to stop the car quickly or change the direction in which the car is moving. Just as Newton predicted, a skidding car continues moving in a straight line. If a tree or another car happens to be in the way of that straight line, there is very little the driver of the skidding car can do except hope that the seat belts are secure and the air bag system works.

Cars equipped with ABS are much less likely to skid when the driver applies the brakes during an emergency. The ABS work by having a sensor at each wheel measure how fast the wheel is changing speeds. If the sensor determines that the wheel is about to lock up and cause a skid, a small computer takes control of the braking system and reduces the pressure being applied to that brake. The wheel doesn't skid, and the driver is still able to steer the car even during an emergency.

Scientists and engineers are working to make cars safer all the time, but no car safety device is perfect. For now, the best advice for any driver or passenger is, "Buckle your lap and shoulder seat belts, and drive carefully." If the car stops suddenly, let the safety belt and the air bag stop your straight-line motion—not the windshield.

When this car drives over the patch of ice, the force of friction between the tires and the road is decreased. The car will begin to skid.

Air bags and seat belts act to control the harmful effects of inertia. But sometimes inertia's effects are exactly what is wanted. Many of the structures that engineers design take advantage of the inertia of certain materials. The more massive an object is, and the more inertia it has, the more it resists being moved. When you want something to stay in place or to hold back a great amount of energy, you make it very massive. Inertia holds earthen dams in place, allowing us to hold water in lakes and control floods. Massive rocks are used to line shipping channels and make jetties. The inertia of the rocks prevents them from being washed away.

Minds On!
Work in groups of four to come up with a list of several examples of structures or products that use inertia to hold back force or protect consumers. Write your lists in your **Activity Log** on page 17. Share your list with the other groups in your class. ●

Sum It Up
In this lesson, you've learned that net forces change the state of motion of an object. A net force on an object exists when the forces acting on it are unbalanced—that is, when the forces acting on the object interact in opposite directions with unequal force. Unless an unbalanced or net force acts on an object, the object will tend to keep doing whatever it is already doing. If the object is at rest, it tends to remain at rest. If the object is moving, it tends to continue moving in a straight line and at a constant speed. You've also learned that inertia is the property of matter that resists changes in the speed or direction of motion. More massive objects have more inertia. When you understand how forces act together on matter, you can answer the questions that began this lesson—"Why does matter sit still? Why does matter keep moving?"

Critical Thinking
1. In your own words, tell what Newton's First Law of Motion means.
2. What is the relationship between mass and inertia?
3. Is it possible for an object to have several forces acting on it and still not change its motion? Why or why not?
4. Is it possible for an object to continue to move if there is no force on it in the direction in which it is moving?
5. What do seat belts in cars have to do with the First Law of Motion?

55

Theme **T** SYSTEMS and INTERACTIONS

What Controls Acceleration?

—moving faster and faster and faster—

—slowing down more and more and more—

—dodging to the right, darting to the left—

Moving faster, slowing down, and changing directions are all examples of acceleration. Why does a baseball accelerate after it leaves the pitcher's hand? Why does a soccer ball slow down when it hits a fence? In this lesson, you'll explore the kinds of things that affect an object's acceleration.

Propellers roar and tires screech. An airplane and a sports car race side by side down a deserted runway. The car pulls even with the airplane. The fearless hero jumps from the car to the airplane, captures the criminal, and . . . the movie ends.

Could a fast car really catch an airplane before the plane takes off, or is the scene just a movie trick? Is there a scientific way to

compare the speeds of an airplane and a car and predict what will happen? One way to approach this question is to use what you've already learned about measuring an object's motion. In order to figure out if the car can really keep up with the plane, you need to know how far the airplane rolls down the runway and how fast it's moving when it lifts off the ground. In other words, you need to know about the plane's change of position and the plane's acceleration.

Minds On! Can a car accelerate as fast as this airplane? Absolutely! Many sports cars can reach speeds of 160 kilometers (about 100 miles) per hour in about 660 meters (2,200 feet). Drag-racing cars can accelerate to 400 kilometers (about 250 miles) per hour in about 440 meters (about 1,465 feet).

By applying your present knowledge of how objects move, can you tell if a chase scene is really happening the way it appears in a movie? •

Twin-engine airplanes like the one shown need to roll about 660 meters (2,200 feet) down the runway in order to reach their takeoff speed of 160 kilometers (about 100 miles) per hour. A car must be able to reach the same speed within the same distance in order for someone to leap from it to the plane.

EXPLORE Activity!

Rolling Along With a Constant Force

Let's explore what causes a change in an object's acceleration.

What You Need

roller skate
string, 1 m
newton spring scale
3 2-L plastic soft-drink bottles/caps
smooth surface — 1 m long
2 L of water
Sand — enough to fill a 2-L bottle
Activity Log pages 18–19

What To Do

1. Fill a 2-L bottle with water. Leave the second 2-L bottle empty. Fill the third 2-L bottle with sand. Screw the caps on all the bottles.

2. Place the bottle of water on the skate. Attach the skate to the spring scale with a piece of string. Gently pull on the spring scale until you apply just enough force to start the skate and bottle moving very slowly.

What Now? Step 2 ▶

3 How many newtons of force did you use to move the bottle of water? Record the data in your **Activity Log**.

4 Remove the bottle of water and place the empty bottle on the skate. Attach the spring scale as before and pull just hard enough to start the skate and empty bottle moving very slowly. Compare the amount of force needed to move the empty bottle to the amount of force needed in step 2. Record your comparison in your **Activity Log**. Leave the empty bottle on the skate. Hold the skate still with one hand. Pull the spring scale until it shows the same amount of force that you used to move the bottle of water in step 2. Keep pulling on the scale with the same amount of force you used to move the bottle of water. Now, let go of the skate. Record your observations in your **Activity Log**.

What Happened?

1. Which has more mass—the empty bottle or the bottle of water?
2. Which takes more force to accelerate—the empty bottle or the bottle of water?
3. When you apply the same amount of force to each bottle, which one accelerates more, the empty bottle or the bottle of water?

What Now?

1. The bottle of sand has more mass and therefore more inertia or resistance to change in motion than either the empty bottle or bottle of water. How much force do you think it would take to accelerate the bottle of sand?
2. Set up an experiment to test your prediction of the amount of force needed to move the bottle of sand. Was your prediction correct?
3. Why do bicycle racers use very low-mass bicycles? Would a bicycle with a large amount of inertia help win a race?

EXPLORE

A Relationship—Pushes and Pulls, Mass, and Acceleration

A large force applied to this soccer ball will cause a large acceleration of the soccer ball.

In the Explore Activity, you saw that more massive objects require more force to accelerate. The water-filled bottle required more force to accelerate than the empty bottle did. The water-filled bottle had more mass than the empty bottle. The sand-filled bottle had more mass than the water-filled bottle. The sand-filled bottle required more force to accelerate than the water-filled bottle. If you think about it, you experience this relationship every day.

Since we expect matter to move in predictable ways, we plan our actions to suit our predictions about motion. You wouldn't play a game of tennis with a bowling ball or try to knock down a brick wall with a feather.

The force of the foot on this soccer ball causes the ball to accelerate.

A small force applied to this soccer ball will cause a small acceleration of the soccer ball.

Yet feathers and bowling balls are both matter. Recall that all matter is composed of atoms, and atoms are composed of electrons, protons, and neutrons. All matter moves according to the Laws of Motion discovered by Sir Isaac Newton.

Also recall that a force is a push or a pull that one object exerts on another object. Newton's Second Law of Motion states the relationship among pushes and pulls, mass, and acceleration. The Second Law of Motion states—

The acceleration of an object depends on the net force acting on that object and on the mass of that object.

If the mass of an object does not change, the acceleration of the object will increase when a larger force is applied. For example, when you tap a soccer ball with your toe, it hardly moves. Kick it hard, however, and the soccer ball flies down the field.

If the force exerted on two objects is the same, the acceleration of the object with the larger mass will be less than the acceleration of the object with the smaller mass. Race cars are built from very light materials. If two cars are identical except for their masses and the same amount of force is applied by the cars' engines, the race car with the lower mass will accelerate faster than the race car with the greater mass.

When engineers design an automobile, they can use the relationships among mass, force, and acceleration given in Newton's Second Law to predict how the car will perform. During the design stage, engineers may decide to build a car using low-mass or high-mass materials, or they may put a larger engine in the car to produce more force.

An animal, however, doesn't have the option of redesigning itself to improve its ability to accelerate. Once an animal is grown up, its abilities to run, jump, and change direction don't change very much. Yet an animal's speed and mobility can mean the difference between life and death.

Have you ever tried to catch a grasshopper? When a grasshopper sitting on a blade of grass sees you approaching, it uses its big hind legs to spring into the air and fly away. Every time it lands, it uses its hind legs to produce the force required to send it flying off in a different direction.

Grasshopper legs can't produce a large amount of force. But grasshoppers have to be able to escape from bigger, stronger, faster animals including birds, toads, and people. The rela-

This baseball pitcher is exerting a force to accelerate the baseball. The catcher's mitt is well padded to absorb the force of the accelerating baseball.

tionships among a grasshopper's mass, the force it can produce, and its rate of acceleration help to explain how it can avoid being captured.

Grasshoppers are hard to catch because of their

great ability to accelerate. They have a small amount of mass, so the small amount of force they can produce with their legs and wings is enough to accelerate them to top speed very quickly. Having low mass also allows grasshoppers to change directions almost instantly. Recall that changing direction while moving is also acceleration.

Many other animals also depend on changing directions quickly to help assure their survival. Fleas, frogs, and houseflies are all super accelerators. All of them are low in mass, can go from a standstill to top speed very quickly, and can change directions in a flash. They're living proof that races are not always won by the fastest competitor. Sometimes the best accelerator wins.

Momentum

If you play baseball or hockey, you probably wear a helmet and pads. These protect you if you're hit by the ball or puck. But tennis players don't need to wear pads or a helmet. Tennis balls travel as fast or faster than baseballs, but getting hit by one usually doesn't cause serious injuries. Why do baseballs and hockey pucks hurt when they hit you? You can use Newton's Second Law of Motion to answer this question. First, a baseball has more mass than a tennis ball. Also, changing the speed of a baseball from a large value to zero (or slowing down) requires a large negative acceleration. The force your body must exert to cause this negative acceleration increases as the mass of the ball increases. The greater force required to stop a baseball compared to a tennis ball is enough to cause severe injury. This is why baseball catchers wear padded catcher's mitts. The padded catcher's mitt absorbs most of the force from the moving baseball. The catcher's hand doesn't need to exert all of the force to slow down and stop the baseball, and the catcher won't experience pain or injury to his or her hand.

But acceleration is hard to measure. Sometimes what you really want to know about a moving object is "Is it going to cause damage if it hits me at that speed?" In other words, how much "bashing power" does it have?

Do the next activity to learn about "bashing power."

This grasshopper uses its hind legs to produce the force that accelerates it forward.

63

TRY THIS Activity!

Does It Bounce or Does It Bash?

Which do you think has more "bashing power"—a table-tennis ball or a golf ball moving at the same velocity? Do this activity to find out.

What You Need
golf ball, table-tennis ball, large, empty coffee can—open on one end, rubber band, 2 paper tissues, goggles, *Activity Log* page 20

Hold a table-tennis ball in one hand and a golf ball in the other. Hold both balls 1 m above the floor. Release both of them at exactly the same time. They'll hit the floor at the same instant. Are they traveling at the same speed when they hit the floor? How can you tell?

Place a paper tissue on top of the open end of a large, empty can. Hold it in place with the rubber band so that it's tight like a drumhead. Hold the table-tennis ball 1 m above the can and drop it so that the ball hits the middle of the tissue. (If the ball doesn't hit the center of the tissue, try again.) What happens?

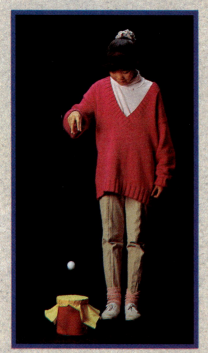

Place a new paper tissue on top of the open end of the can as you did before. Hold the golf ball 1 m above the can and drop it so the ball hits the middle of the tissue. (If the ball doesn't hit the center of the tissue, try again.) What happens this time? Which ball has more "bashing power?" Record your answers in your *Activity Log*.

"Bashing Power" is Momentum!

Scientists have a term that means "bashing power." They call it momentum. **Momentum** (mō men′ təm) is defined as the product of an object's velocity times its mass. You probably already know that getting hit by a massive object (like a car) or getting hit by a fast-moving object (like a baseball) will hurt. An object's "bashing power" depends on its mass times its velocity, or its momentum. Think about momentum as you debate about bicycle helmet laws on page 65.

> **Momentum is defined as the product of an object's velocity times its mass.**

64

A bicycle safety helmet protects its wearer's head from injury in the event of an accident.

SCIENCE TECHNOLOGY AND Society

Bicycle Helmet Laws

How much momentum do you have as you ride a bicycle down the street? Your mass doesn't change as you ride along, but often your velocity increases (you accelerate). As your velocity increases, your momentum increases—you have more "bashing power."

What happens if you fall from your bicycle with this greater "bashing power?" You would probably injure yourself! Approximately 1,000 Americans die each year as a result of bicycle accidents. The cause of death is head trauma in 75 percent of these accidents.

Lawmakers in some areas of the United States have passed bills requiring all bicyclists to wear helmets or pay fines—as much as $100 per violation. The makers of these laws realize that the greater "bashing power" a bicycle rider's head has, the greater the risk of injury to the head.

Many bicycle riders don't want to wear helmets. They think helmets are hot and uncomfortable. These "anti-helmet" bicycle riders feel that laws shouldn't require them to wear safety helmets if they don't want to.

What do you think? Get together with several of your classmates who have different opinions on bicycle helmet laws. Have a debate about the pros and cons of bicycle safety helmet laws.

The Momentum of Space Junk

Would you believe that a piece of aluminum the size of a pencil eraser could cause as much damage to an orbiting space shuttle as a bomb? It's true! Over a million tiny pieces of "space trash" consisting of flecks of paint, plastic, and small pieces of metal from old satellites are orbiting Earth at very high velocities. Many pieces are in orbits where they may hit the space shuttle or other satellites. The momentum of this trash is so large that space scientists and astronauts are worried about the potential danger it poses.

This is a scanning electron micrograph of a crater in the louvers of a space satellite. The satellite had been exposed to space for about 50 months. Scientists found six holes per square foot of the louvers. These craters were caused by very high velocity impacts with paint flakes.

Pieces of space trash in orbit may hit orbiting satellites like this one.

Most of the pieces of space trash are very small—no bigger than this letter "o." But these small pieces of junk are moving at extremely high velocities— about 11,200 meters (about 7 miles) per second. These objects have a small mass, but because of the high velocities at which they are moving, they have an enormous amount of momentum.

In 1983, the windshield of a space shuttle was hit by a fleck of paint smaller than the dot over this letter "i." This paint particle gouged a small crater in the window. If the window had broken, the spacecraft might have been destroyed during reentry.

The National Aeronautics and Space Administration (NASA) is concerned about the dangers caused by space trash. NASA is sponsoring research on ways to avoid damage caused by these tiny bits of orbiting junk. Someday we may launch a space-traveling, garbage-collecting satellite to make space travel safer!

Literature Link

Burton's Zoom Zoom Va-ROOOM Machine

How do people come up with ideas such as a space-traveling, garbage-collecting satellite? Usually ideas such as this come from a need that someone has identified.

"Where do ideas come from, anyway? Burton didn't know. They just happened.

Sometimes he saw a problem that cried out for an answer, like poor Clinton's misery. That had resulted in the Automatic Dog-Washing Machine.

Sometimes he just wished things didn't have to be the way they were—like having to make his bed every morning. And so his No-Hands Automatic BedMaking Machine came to be.

Sometimes his ideas grew out of things he seemed to see in snow swirling in the wind or in the shadowy lines of a tree.

There were more ideas around than Burton could possibly use. It was only when he saw a really great one that he glommed onto it and set to work. He worked fast, never able to catch up with his excitement.

There was no way Burton could have guessed the astonishing idea that was waiting for him to find it that particular day."
(excerpted from *Burton's Zoom Zoom Va-ROOOM Machine* by Dorothy Haas)

Read about Burton's ideas. Have you ever invented anything? Whether you have or not, where do you think ideas come from? Brainstorm with one or two classmates to decide on a problem that needs a solution. Then come up with several ideas to solve it. The ideas don't have to be practical or even possible. Just make them creative.

Applying the Second Law of Motion

How has Newton's Second Law of Motion changed the way we live? Let's look at some more creative ideas in the fields of medical and sports engineering.

Roger jogged three kilometers this afternoon. Lots of people do that, but Roger does it while wearing two artificial legs made of carbon fiber, the space-age metal titanium (tī tā′ nē əm), and a new type of plastic. These strong, low-mass materials of which his artificial legs are made have helped Roger lead a much more active life.

Roger's legs were badly injured in a car crash. It was necessary to amputate them. He was fitted with a pair of wooden legs and learned to walk again. But the wooden legs were heavy. After walking a few blocks, he would need to rest. The Second Law of Motion helps explain why Roger's new legs are so much easier to use than the more massive older set.

Roger's use of low-mass artificial legs has allowed him to accelerate faster than when he used heavier wooden artificial legs.

When you are walking or running, the muscles of your thighs and hips apply a force to your lower legs. This causes your lower legs and feet to accelerate. The more massive your foot and lower leg is, the more force is required to move them forward quickly.

Roger's thigh and hip muscles can produce only a limited amount of force. When these muscles are applying their maximum force to a large mass, they get tired quickly. By switching to artificial legs made of less massive materials, Roger was able to reduce the mass that his muscles had to accelerate with each step. Using low-mass artificial legs allowed Roger to accelerate faster than when he used the heavier wooden legs with the same maximum amount of force.

Reducing the mass of sports equipment can also improve other athletes' performances. Imagine how hard it would be to run a 10-kilometer (6.2-mile) race with a brick strapped to each of your shoes! Competitive runners wear low-mass racing shoes for the same reason that Roger benefitted from low-mass artificial legs.

Runners can accelerate more quickly in low-mass shoes. In a long race, low-mass shoes are less tiring to wear. Running shoes need to provide a balance between low mass and adequate protection for the runners' feet, however. Sports shoes are designed to protect the runner's feet from injuries and to spring off the running surface, allowing the runner to bounce a little on each stride. If the mass is too low, foot protection is sacrificed.

Looking Back

Remember the race between the airplane and the sports car? The sports car accelerated at about the same rate as the airplane. Now can you use the Second Law of Motion to explain how they accelerated at about the same rate?

Sum It Up

In this lesson, you've been studying Newton's Second Law of Motion and learning how forces, mass, and acceleration act in relationship to each other. Newton's Second Law of Motion states that the acceleration of an object depends on the force applied to it and on the mass of the object. You've seen Newton's Second Law at work when you exerted a force to accelerate a roller skate with different amounts of mass on it. You've also studied the relationship among force, mass, and acceleration in the real world—in cars and planes, in sports, and in insects and other animals jumping to save their lives. Momentum is the product of mass times velocity. Momentum can be thought of as "bashing power." You experienced the effects of mass times velocity or "bashing power" when you dropped a golf ball and a table-tennis ball onto a paper tissue. The harmful interactions that take place when one massive object hits another can be prevented or reduced by the use of helmets, seat belts, and air bags. Whether the forces, masses, and accelerations that are acting together on an object are great or small, Newton's Second Law always governs what happens.

Critical Thinking

1. In your own words, explain Newton's Second Law of Motion.
2. Why do some sports cars accelerate quickly?
3. If a tennis ball and a baseball are moving at the same velocity, which has more momentum? Why?
4. A baseball player found that she could hit the ball farther when she used a heavier bat. However, when she tried an even heavier bat, she didn't hit the ball as far. Why do you think this happened?
5. Why does it take more force to pedal a bicycle to get it started moving than when you are already bicycling along a level street?

Theme — **SYSTEMS and INTERACTIONS**

What Are Action and Reaction Forces?

Action and reaction pairs. What do these words have to do with forces? What interaction occurs between two objects that causes an action and a reaction? If you push your hand against the wall, does the wall push back against your hand? In this lesson, you'll explore how forces always exist in action and reaction pairs.

Struggling to control the fire hose, a team of firefighters advances toward a solid wall of flames. The fire and smoke are dangerous, but so is the force exerted by the fire hose. No single firefighter is strong enough to control the force exerted by this large fire hose. The hose pushes backward against the firefighters. They must work as a team to push the hose forward toward the fire. If the wiggling hose escapes their grasp, it may whip around and seriously injure a member of the team.

Dangling over the edge of a cliff, a rock climber's safety depends on her climbing skill and on the rope to which she is attached. The upward force exerted on the climber by the rope is saving her from falling. Climbers inspect their ropes carefully before each use. What might happen if a sharp rock sliced partway through the rope? Do the next activity to look at action and reaction forces.

The firefighters must work as a team to push the hose toward the fire.

TRY THIS Activity!

Wheeling Away!

Let's experience pairs of forces.

What You Need
desk chair on wheels, 2–L plastic bottle, sand, *Activity Log* page 21

Sit on the desk chair and push against the wall with your foot. Did you and the chair change positions? How far did you travel? In what direction did you move? Can you name the pairs of forces?

Return the chair to its original position, and this time push harder against the wall. When you push against the wall, do you feel the wall pushing back against your foot? Now move the chair away from the wall. Clear a large space in front of and behind the chair. Fill the 2–L bottle with sand. Sit in the chair with both feet a few inches off the floor and hold the sand-filled bottle in front of your chest. Using both hands, push the bottle away from your body and release it.

Safety Tip: Be sure no one is close enough to be hit by the bottle!

How did you apply a force to the bottle? Did the bottle apply a force to you? Did the chair move when you released the bottle? Record your observations in your *Activity Log.*

Minds On!

Have you ever filled a balloon with air and let it go? What happened? Does it take a force to fill a balloon with air? How can you tell? Does the air inside a balloon exert a force against the rubber sides of the balloon? How can you tell? Do the rubber sides of the balloon exert a force against the air inside? How can you tell? Why does the balloon fly around the room when you let go of the open end? What forces are acting on the balloon and on the air?•

According to Sir Isaac Newton, seeing an apple falling from a tree stimulated his thinking and led to his discovering what we now call Newton's Laws of Motion.

You already know about Newton's First and Second Laws. These laws explain how unbalanced forces affect the motion of matter. Now you'll explore Newton's Third Law of Motion.

This climber exerts a downward force on the rope.

71

EXPLORE Activity!

Launching a Balloon-Powered Rocket

Let's build and test a rocket that uses a balloon for its engine.

What You Need

balloon
long thin plastic bag
plastic drinking straw
4 m of string
masking tape (2 pieces, each about 8 cm long)
meterstick
2 chairs
Activity Log pages 22–23

What To Do

1. Tie one end of the string to the back of a chair or desk. Push the string through the drinking straw. Tie the other end of the string to a second chair. Move the chairs apart until the string is level and tight.

2. Tape the plastic bag to the straw as shown. Blow up the balloon and hold the end closed. Don't tie a knot in the end!

3. Pull the straw and plastic bag to one end of the string so that the open end of the plastic bag is at the knot in the string. Place the balloon inside the plastic bag and let go. What do you observe? Use the meterstick to measure the distance traveled.

4 Have the same student blow up the balloon again. Place the balloon inside the plastic bag and fly the balloon-powered rocket along the string again. Repeat this process 4 more times. Measure the distances traveled with the meterstick. Record your measurements and observations in your **Activity Log**. Calculate the average distance traveled.

What Happened?

1. How far did the balloon rocket travel along the string? What was the average distance traveled by the balloon rocket?
2. What pushes the air out of the balloon? Would the straw travel along the string if you attached a paper bag full of air to the straw and then let go? Why or why not?
3. What do you think caused your balloon-powered rocket to move in the direction it did?

What Now?

1. How can you measure the average speed of the balloon?
2. Help your teacher organize a balloon rocket race. How could you make your balloon-powered rocket go faster? Can you make it travel completely across the room?

Equal and Opposite Forces

Gases expanding

Nozzle opens; expanding gases escape

Newton asked himself, "Where do forces come from?" He realized that forces always come in pairs that are equal and act in opposite directions. The apple he may have seen hanging from a tree was pulling down against the limb of the tree. The limb, on the other hand, was pulling up against the weight of the apple. These upward and downward forces were opposite and equal. Newton decided that a force applied to any object must be applied by another object. Newton was able to then state his Third Law of Motion—

Whenever an object exerts a force on a second object, the second object exerts an equal and opposite force on the first object.

The force of the expanding gases escaping through the nozzle of the rocket is the action force.

This law can be stated in terms of action and reaction forces—**for every action force, there is an equal but opposite reaction force.** It's important to note that the "action" force and the "reaction" force are acting on different objects.

Both balloon-powered rockets and rockets traveling in outer space provide good examples of equal and opposite action-reaction forces. The stretched balloon pushes on the air, forcing it out of the open end of the balloon. This is the action force. An equal and opposite reaction force occurs inside the balloon as the air pushes back on the balloon. This reaction force pushes the straw forward along the string.

Rocket boosters attached to the space shuttle push it into orbit in the same way. When the space shuttle's rocket boosters are started, they burn fuel and produce large amounts of hot gases that rush out of the back of the booster. That's the action force. The reaction force of the gases pushing back on the booster is equal in strength but opposite in direction. This reaction force sends the shuttle and rocket boosters upward.

Let's look back to some of the examples given in the first part of this lesson and see how the Third Law of Motion explains what's happening.

Remember the fire hose shooting water on the burning building. The nozzle of the fire hose is pushing in the opposite direction from which the water is moving. The force of the water pump pushing water out of the hose produces an action force. The force of the expelled water pushing back against the hose produces the reaction force. The reaction force is exactly equal in strength to the action force but is pointed in the opposite direction. Firefighters are able to hold the hose still by pushing it toward the building with all their strength. They're using their muscles to produce a force that balances the reaction force. As long as the forces on the hose are balanced, the net force on the hose is zero, and the hose doesn't move.

Pairs of action and reaction forces are present whether matter is moving or sitting still. Forces always act in pairs. The rock climber on page 71 dangling in mid-air isn't moving up or down. She is exerting a downward action force on the rope equal to the weight of her body and equipment. The rope is exerting an upward reaction force on the climber. The upward force of the rope on the climber is exactly equal to the downward force exerted by the climber on the rope. However, until an unbalanced force acts on the climber, she will not move up or down.

Action-reaction forces

Action-reaction forces

Mollusk Movers

Action and reaction forces are found in nature as well. Mollusks make up the largest group of water animals. Mollusks are generally slow moving creatures like snails, slugs, scallops, squids, and clams. But several types of mollusks use very specialized action-reaction forces to move around quite rapidly.

Scallops are two-shelled mollusks that look similar to clams. Scallops can change their locations or escape danger by rapidly opening and closing their shells. When a scallop closes its shells, water is forced out from between the shells. The action force is caused by the force of the shells on the water. The scallop then shoots backward. This reaction is caused by the force of the expelled water on the scallop's shells.

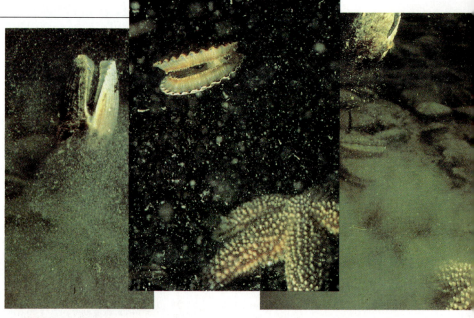

This scallop is using action and reaction forces to escape from the sea star, a predator.

Squids are another type of mollusk that use an even more remarkable scheme for high-speed swimming. Squids are fast-moving hunters that live in the sea. They use their tentacles to swim forward or backward and to grasp the fish they eat. But if a squid is trying to catch a fish to eat (or avoid being eaten by a much bigger fish), it shoots a high-velocity stream of water out of a tube in its body (the action force). The reaction force is caused by the force of the expelled water on the squid. The result of this reaction force is acceleration in the direction opposite to the high-velocity stream of water. Can you see a similarity between the squid and the fire hose?

Squids use action-reaction forces to accelerate rapidly. The funnel tube can be reversed for acceleration in the opposite direction.

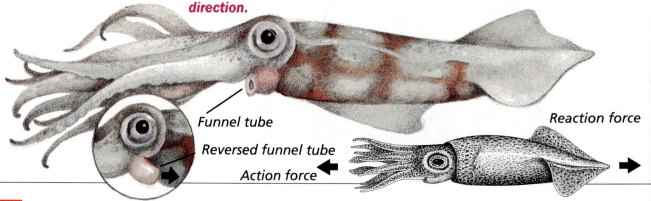

Funnel tube

Reversed funnel tube

Action force

Reaction force

Health Link

If You Provide the Action, What's the Reaction?

All sporting events involve action and reaction forces. Some are very obvious, and some are a bit harder to identify. For example, when you're roller skating and you push against the wall, you're exerting an action force on the wall. The wall exerts an equal and opposite reaction force on you that will accelerate you away from the wall. You can't see the wall moving in the opposite direction, but there is a very small motion of the area of the wall that you pushed against. Another example would be hitting a baseball. You exert an action force with the bat on the ball, but the ball also exerts an equal and opposite reaction force on the bat.

Work in groups of three or four to list as many action-reaction forces in sporting events as you can. Record these sporting events in your **Activity Log** page 24. Trade lists with other groups and discuss these sporting events in class. Remember—action-reaction forces act on different objects!

What are the action and reaction forces in these sporting events?

Each of the action-reaction pairs shown is equal. The net force on the bowling ball is in the upward direction, therefore the bowling ball is accelerated upward.

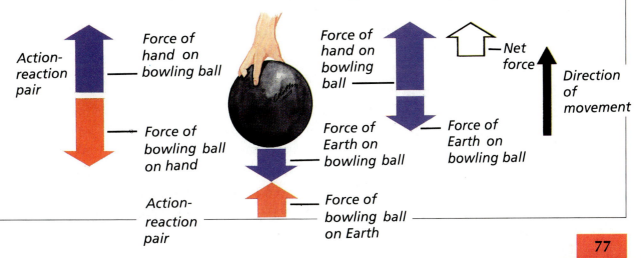

Why Do We Need To Know About the Third Law of Motion?

The Third Law of Motion can help you predict what will happen when you apply a force to an object. This happens daily in your life. For instance, when you push the door to your classroom open, the door will exert a force on your hand. That's why it takes some work to push the door open. You need to overcome the force the door exerts on your hand.

The Third Law of Motion is also important for many technical jobs, such as engineering, architecture, and mechanics. People who work in these fields need to know about action and reaction forces so they can plan how to control all possible forces when doing their jobs.

How does knowing about Newton's Third Law of Motion aid a bridge designer? Do the following activity to find out.

TRY THIS Activity!

Design Your Own Bridge!

Use your knowledge of action and reaction forces to build a model bridge from playing cards.

What You Need
deck of playing cards, masking tape

Work with 2 other students to build a support structure for a bridge that is strong enough to support 2 large textbooks, using only playing cards and masking tape. Rules for building your bridge: You may use no more than 10 playing cards to construct your bridge. You can't use any wood, steel, or other sturdy material to make your bridge stronger. You may use masking tape to hold the structure together.

How you construct the bridge is completely up to your design team. Be creative! Experiment with your design and build something original! Whose bridge will be the strongest? Who will have the most unique design? Which team will use the fewest playing cards to hold up the books? Build yours and find out!

Engineers and architects need to know about action and reaction forces when they design bridges and buildings.

of action forces and reaction forces—"For every action force, there is an equal and opposite reaction force." Remember, action and reaction forces act on different objects. You experienced these forces interacting on matter in your activity with the balloon and straw on a string. You've also explored and read about action and reaction forces in sporting events, space travel, and underwater life. In fact, no two objects anywhere can interact without there being action and reaction forces.

Critical Thinking

1. In your own words, explain Newton's Third Law of Motion.
2. A girl climbs a rope during gym class. She exerts a force on the rope due to her weight. What other force or forces are involved in this situation?
3. What action and reaction pairs exist when catching a basketball?
4. What action and reaction pairs exist when sleeping in a bed?
5. What action and reaction pairs exist when a rocket accelerates into space?

CAREERS

Structural Design Engineers

The Third Law of Motion is very important to structural design engineers. Part of the job of structural design engineers is to design frameworks and foundations for buildings and equipment. If these engineers didn't understand applications of the Third Law of Motion, many engineering decisions would be a matter of guesswork.

To become a structural design engineer, you must study mathematics, physics, and engineering in college. Having a curiosity about forces and motion helps!

Part of the job of structural design engineers is to study what causes structural failures of equipment. The engineers then work out solutions to prevent future breakdowns. Good engineering designs make buildings and equipment safer and more reliable to use. With their knowledge and experience, structural design engineers really make a difference in people's lives!

Sum It Up

Newton's Third Law of Motion says, "For every force, there is an equal and opposite force." This law can also be stated in terms

79

Theme T SYSTEMS and INTERACTIONS

Tug-of-War Contests Revisited

Do you recall the tug-of-war contests shown at the beginning of this unit? Let's apply what we've learned throughout this unit to see who will really win these contests!

Is the force exerted on the rope by the team on the left balanced by the force exerted on the rope by the team on the right? What will have to happen in order for one of the teams to win this tug-of-war contest?

Is the force exerted on the rope by the adult balanced by the force exerted on the rope by the children? What will have to happen for a winner to be declared in this tug-of-war contest?

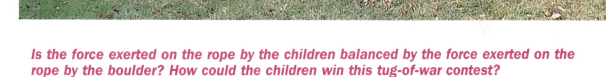

Is the force exerted on the rope by the children balanced by the force exerted on the rope by the boulder? How could the children win this tug-of-war contest?

Is the force exerted on the rope by the children on roller skates balanced by the force exerted on the rope by the children in shoes? What will happen when both teams exert more force on the rope?

Environmental Costs

shares of world energy consumption 1987

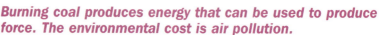

Burning coal produces energy that can be used to produce force. The environmental cost is air pollution.

You've looked at the forces involved in tug-of-war contests, and you've identified where these forces were working and how they interacted with each other and with matter. Now, let's think about other places where forces are important and how they are produced.

Today in the United States, we often use machines to produce the force needed to get us from one place to another or to process the food we eat. The machines use energy in the form of coal, oil, and gas to produce the force. Before many of these machines were invented, however, people used to rely on muscle power to do some of these jobs. Some countries still rely on older forms of producing force.

Burning oil produces energy that can be used to produce force. Oil spills are a possible environmental cost.

These countries use much less of the world's limited fossil-fuel resources to support each person. An average resident of India uses about 50 times less energy than is used by a United States resident.

What are the environmental costs of using so much energy? The costs include air pollution, oil spills, decreasing amounts of ozone in the atmosphere, decreasing numbers of forests on Earth...the list of environmental concerns is long.

Some of the solutions to these concerns lie in making informed decisions about the methods we use to produce force and do work. If you can use your muscles to walk to the library, should you ask someone to drive you there? If a system of mass transportation could be developed in your area, would enough people ride it instead of driving their cars? Walking or riding mass transportation helps to conserve fuel and thereby stretch Earth's limited fuel reserves.

Work with two friends to do the following Try This Activity. How can you use your knowledge of forces to help make a difference in the world?

TRY THIS Activity!

A New Way To Move

Work in groups of 3 to design a new method of transportation. This could be a new type of bicycle, a new type of car, a new type of boat, or whatever you decide. Try to make your new method of transportation use energy efficiently. Brainstorm to come up with several ideas, then choose the best idea and test it. Use what you now know about forces—frictional forces, gravitational forces, balanced and unbalanced forces, and action and reaction forces—to help with your design. Share responsibility for gathering background information and equipment, then work together to build your transportation model. Share your model with your classmates.

83

GLOSSARY

Use the pronunciation key below to help you decode, or read, the pronunciations.

Pronunciation Key

a	at, bad		d	dear, soda, bad
ā	ape, pain, day, break		f	five, defend, leaf, off, cough, elephant
ä	father, car, heart		g	game, ago, fog, egg
âr	care, pair, bear, their, where		h	hat, ahead
e	end, pet, said, heaven, friend		hw	white, whether, which
ē	equal, me, feet, team, piece, key		j	joke, enjoy, gem, page, edge
i	it, big, English, hymn		k	kite, bakery, seek, tack, cat
ī	ice, fine, lie, my		l	lid, sailor, feel, ball, allow
îr	ear, deer, here, pierce		m	man, family, dream
o	odd, hot, watch		n	not, final, pan, knife
ō	old, oat, toe, low		ng	long, singer, pink
ô	coffee, all, taught, law, fought		p	pail, repair, soap, happy
ôr	order, fork, horse, story, pour		r	ride, parent, wear, more, marry
oi	oil, toy		s	sit, aside, pets, cent, pass
ou	out, now		sh	shoe, washer, fish mission, nation
u	up, mud, love, double		t	tag, pretend, fat, button, dressed
ū	use, mule, cue, feud, few		th	thin, panther, both
ü	rule, true, food		th	this, mother, smooth
ù	put, wood, should		v	very, favor, wave
ûr	burn, hurry, term, bird, word, courage		w	wet, weather, reward
ə	about, taken, pencil, lemon, circus		y	yes, onion
b	bat, above, job		z	zoo, lazy, jazz, rose, dogs, houses
ch	chin, such, match		zh	vision, treasure, seizure

acceleration (ak sel′ ə ra′ shən): the rate at which velocity changes

action-reaction pairs (ak′ shən-re ak′ shən): two forces, acting on different bodies, having equal strength but opposite direction

air resistance (âr ri zis′ təns): the force of air against a moving object; also called drag

average speed: the total distance an object travels divided by the total time it takes to travel the distance

balanced forces (bal′ ənsed fôrs ez): forces, acting on the same body, equal in size but opposite in direction

constant speed (kon′ stənt spēd): no change in speed

drag: see air resistance

force: a push or pull one body exerts on another

friction (frik′ shən): a force that opposes motion between two surfaces that are touching each other

gravity (grav′ i tē): the mutual force of attraction that exists between all objects in the universe, force Earth exerts on all objects on or near it

hypothesis (hī poth′ ə sis): the proposed answer to a question or tentative solution to a problem; should be testable

inertia (in ûr′ shə): the property of a body that resists any change in velocity

kinetic energy (ki net′ ik en′ ər jē): energy of motion

magnet: any object that has a magnetic field and is able to exert forces on other magnets

mass: the amount of matter in an object; the measure of the inertia of a body

matter: anything that has mass and takes up space

momentum (mō men′ təm): the mass of an object multiplied by its velocity

motion (mō′ shən): change in position

negative acceleration (neg′ ə tiv ak sell ə rā′ shən): the rate of decrease in velocity

net force: force that results from unbalanced forces acting on an object; changes the motion of an object

newton (N) (nū′ tən): the unit of force; force required to accelerate a 1-kg mass at the rate 1 m/s/s

physicists (fiz′ ə sists): scientists who study the structure and interaction of matter, as well as the changes in position that matter undergoes

plates: rigid blocks of Earth's crust and upper mantle

potential (pə ten′ shəl) **energy:** the energy of objects due to their position or condition

spring scale: a device used to measure force

unbalanced forces (un bal′ ənsed fôrs′ ez): forces, acting on the same body, unequal in size and/or opposite in direction

velocity (və los′ i tē): the speed and direction of a moving object

weight: the force of gravity that Earth exerts on an object resting on its surface

INDEX

Abu 'l Fath Al-Khazini, 48–49
Acceleration, 21; 56–69; *act.,* 58–59
Action and reaction forces, 70–79
Adkins, Jan, 10, 38
Air bags, 53
Air resistance, 35; *act.,* 35
Analyze, 8
Antilock brakes, 53
Aristotle, 48; *illus.,* 48

Balanced forces, 45; *illus.,* 45
Burton's Zoom Zoom Va-ROOOM Machine **(Haas),** 11, 67

Conclusion, 9
Constant speed, 20

Distance, 16–17
Drag, 35

Energy, environmental costs of using, 82–83; *act.,* 83; potential and kinetic, 50–55
Experiment, 8

Force, 25–39, *act.,* 27, 28–29, 37; action and reaction, 70–79, *act.,* 71, 72–73; net, 44, 45
Friction, 30, 31, 32, 38–39; *act.,* 31; *illus.,* 30, 38; and the environment, 32

Gravity, 34–37, *illus.,* 34

Haas, Dorothy, 11, 67
Halley, Edmund, 48
Helmet Laws, 65
Hidden World of Forces, The **(White),** 11
Hypothesis, 8, 9
Haines, Gail Kaye, 11

Inertia, 46–47, 55; Law of, 46

Kinetic energy, 51

Law of Motion, Newton's First, 46, 52–55; Newton's Second, 60–69; application, 68–69; Newton's Third, 74–79; application, 78, 79; *act.,* 78

Macaulay, David, 11
Matter, 17; in motion, 18–22
Mo-Tzu, 48–49; *illus.,* 49
Momentum, 63–67; *act.,* 64
Motion, 12–23, 40–55; *act.,* 14–15, 20, 41, 42–43; in animals, *table,* 22–23; matter in, 18–22; measuring, 16–17; Newton's First Law, 46, 52–55; Newton's Second Law, 60–69, application, 68–69; Newton's Third Law, 74–79; application, 78, 79; *act.,* 78
Moving Heavy Things **(Adkins),** 10, 38

Net force, 44, 45; *act.,* 44
Newton, 35
Newton, Sir Isaac, 46, 47, 48, 49, 61; *illus.,* 48, 49
Newton's First Law of Motion, 46, 52–55
Newton's Second Law of Motion, 60–69; application, 68–69
Newton's Third Law of Motion, 74–79; application, 78–79; *act.,* 78

Physicist, 17
Plates, 26. *illus.,* 27
Potential energy, 51
Problem, 8

Reaction, and action forces, 70–79

Scientific development, 48–49
Scientific method, 8, 9
Sleds, 39; *illus.,* 39
Space debris, 66–67
Speed, 16, 17; constant, 20; *table,* 22, 23

INDEX continued

Structural design engineers, 79

Time, 16
Travel Agents, 17

Unbalanced forces, 45

Velocity, 18, 19

Way Things Work, The (Macaulay), 11
Which Way Is Up? (Haines), 11
White, Jack R., 11

CREDITS

Photo Credits:
cover, ©L.D. Gordon/The Image Bank; **1,** ©Gary Rosenquist/Earth Images/1980; **3,** (t) ©Studiohio/1991; (b) ©Ron Kimball; **6-9,** ©Fredrik Marsh; **10-11,** ©Studiohio; **12,** ©John P. Kelly/ The Image Bank; **13,** (l) ©Gerard Vandystadt/ Photo Researchers; (r) ©Warren Morgan/Westlight; **14,** ©Doug Martin; **16,** ©Mitchell Reibel/Sportschrome/1990; **18,** (it) ©Tim DeFrisco/Allsport; (ib) ©Indianapolis Motor Speedway; **18-19,** ©Ken Levine/Allsport; **20,** ©Brent Turner/BLT Productions/1991; **22,** (cl) ©R. Newman/The Image Bank/1990; (tr) ©Willi Dolder/Tony Stone Worldwide; **23,** ©Tony Duffy/Allsport/1984; **24,** Gary Rosenquist/Earth Images/1980; **25,** (t) ©Chuck Tonn/USDA Forest Service; (b) ©Jim Quiring/USDA Forest Service; **26,** ©Peter Willing; **28,** ©Ken Karp for MMSD; **30,** ©Studiohio; (i) ©Gary Gay/The Image Bank/1984; **33,** (t) ©Vic Bider/The Stock Market; (bl) ©Michael Hans/Photo Researchers, Inc.; (br) ©Doug Martin/1991; **34,** (r) ©Studiohio; (i) ©Arthur Grace/Stock Boston; **35,** ©Studiohio/1991; **36,** ©NASA/Science Source/Photo Researchers, Inc.; **37,** ©K. Kai/Fujifotos/The Image Works; **38,** ©General Motors; **39,** (i) ©Joe Rychetnik/Photo Researchers, Inc.; (r) ©Charles Campbell/Westlight; **40,** ©Vandystadt/Allsport; **42-43,** ©Studiohio; **44,** ©Fredrik Marsh; (i) ©Studiohio; **46-47,** ©Culver Pictures; **48,** (t) FPG International; (b) North Wind Picture Archives; **49,** (tl) The Bettmann Archive; (tr) Historical Picture Service; **50,** ©W. Bacon/Photo Researchers, Inc.; (i) James Balog/Tony Stone Worldwide; **52,** ©Doug Martin/1991; **53,** ©Chrysler Corporation; **56,** ©Ron Kimball; **57,** ©Jacques Cochin/The Image Bank; **58,** ©Brent Turner/BLT Productions/1991; **60,** (t) ©Janeart LTD/The Image Bank; (b) ©Focus on Sports; **61,** ©Bob Daemmrich/1991; **62,** ©Lon Yamaguchi/Allsport; **63-64,** ©Studiohio; **65,** ©Bob Daemmrich/1991; **66,** ©NASA/Dan McCoy/The Stock Market; **68,** ©Chuck O'Rear/Westlight; **70,** ©Kolvoord/The Image Works; **71,** ©Dave Black/Sportschrome; **72-73,** Studiohio; **74,** ©Hank Morgan/Photo Researchers, Inc.; **76,** ©H.W. Pratt/Biological Photo Service; **77,** (t) ©Simon Bruty/Allsport/1991; (b) ©Don Carroll/The Image Bank/1984; **78,** (l) ©Michael J. Howell/Stock Imagery; (cb) ©Joan Lebold Cohen/Photo Researchers, Inc.; (ct) ©Travelpix/FPG; **79,** ©Chris Rogers/Stock Imagery; **80-81,** ©Fredrik Marsh; **82,** ©Bill Ross/Westlight; **83,** (t) ©Sam Pierson, Jr./Photo Researchers.

Illustration Credits:
22, 23, 27, 48 (m), 49 Anne Rhodes; **27 (t), 51,** Ebet Dudley; **27 (m), 55,** John Edwards; **32, 56, 57, 74,** James Shough; **38, 39, 76 (b),** Susan Moore; **20, 21, 45, 63 (bl),** David Reed; **46, 47,** Jean Probert; **62, 63, 76 (m),** Pam Johnson; **75, 82,** Ann Larson